"This book gives us a rare glimpse into the real-life struggles and triumphs of a life of service. The power and authenticity of these stories is evidence of the great work that God is doing everyday in the lives of his people, not only in the orphans who are being served, but also in those who are called to this incredible ministry. The lessons from these accounts are a reminder of the God who is relentless in the pursuit of his children's hearts."
—MARK SCHULTZ, DOVE AWARD-WINNING RECORDING ARTIST

"Beth's heart to care for the forgotten children of this world has led her on the exciting journey of seeing lives changed and the 'precious extracted from the worthless.' This book is filled with real-life stories of redemption that will leave you both encouraged and challenged. Encouraged to see God at work in all things, and challenged to roll up your sleeves and do something."
—MATTHEW WEST, SINGER/SONGWRITER

"In Relentless Hope, Beth illuminates how God moves in the lives of orphans and spiritual orphans, doing a supernatural work to restore what is broken. As we join God in his work, we find that ministry is about much more than meeting needs, it's about transformation by the power of the Spirit—to see not as the world sees, but to experience the reality of his grace."
—PAUL PENNINGTON, EXECUTIVE DIRECTOR AND CO-FOUNDER, HOPE FOR ORPHANS

EXTRACTING THE PRECIOUS

RELENTLESS

FROM THE WORTHLESS

HOPE

BETH GUCKENBERGER

Standard®
PUBLISHING

Cincinnati, Ohio

Published by Standard Publishing, Cincinnati, Ohio
www.standardpub.com

Printed in: United States of America
Acquisitions editor: Dale Reeves; Project editor: Laura Derico
Cover photo: Zach Nachazel; Author photo: Kristina Gehring, kphoto+design
Cover design: Metaleap Design, Inc.; Interior design: Dina Sorn at Ahaa! Design
Interior photos: pp. 53, 125, 175, Brian Bertke; 161, Ashley Betscher; 29, 68, 92, 229,
Brian Burgdorf; 56, 170, Dan Davis; 163, 200, 203, Andy Ellison; 134, Beth Guckenberger;
102, Kari Johnsen Gydé; 83, Shane Harden; 221, Kevin Judy; 78, Chelsie Puterbaugh; 99,
177, Chris Ramos; 111, Claire Rogers; 40, Dave Schreier; 122, Mark Shaw; 35, Lisa Stanken;
34, 75, 144, 151, 216, Cheryl Weaver

Though all the stories told in this book are true, some of the names and details have been
changed in order to protect those involved.

ISBN 978-0-7847-3178-9

Library of Congress Cataloging-in-Publication Data

Guckenberger, Beth, 1972-
  Relentless hope : extracting the precious from the worthless / Beth Guckenberger.
     p. cm.
  ISBN 978-0-7847-3178-9 (perfect bound)
  1. Hope--Religious aspects--Christianity. 2. Suffering--Religious aspects--Christianity. I.
Title.
  BV4638.G79 2011
  248.8'6--dc22

                              2010048771

16 15 14 13 12 11   1 2 3 4 5 6 7 8 9

TO TODD,
who has taught me about *relentless*.

RELENTLESS

CONTENTS

ACKNOWLEDGMENTS

I always read the acknowledgments before I begin the first page of any book—I like hearing the author's voice when he or she is just "talking," not teaching or preaching or practicing. So here are my acknowledgments with the thought in mind that someone might want to hear about my supportive relationships.

First of all I want to thank the brave people who shared their stories. Some of those meetings were hard, and over and over I was struck by the grace that comes through fire. I am praying, like you, that your "testimony of the process" ministers to others.

I want to thank our incredible Back2Back Ministries staff team, all over the world and in the US. You each have volumes of stories you have lived yourselves, beside those of the ones God has brought into your ministry. I am grateful we minister on your team! Continue the friction . . .

It takes a team to write a book, so thank you, Standard Publishing team: Lindsay, Dale, Sarah, Laura, and all of the other supporting players. The attention you gave me and the respect with which you treated this subject spoke volumes to me about your company's values. Thank you, Angie, for making this connection!

Thank you, Mom, for always listening to my stories and making me feel like they were the best part of your day. You and Dad built a family that loves each other and the world. So, Brad and Chris, Ben and Sara, Caroline, Caleb, Abby, Asher, Rose, Sophia, Jackson, and Courtney, it is so fun to be in the cheering section of your lives. *Cousin* is our favorite word.

To my favorite in-law family, thank you for making me feel like I have always been there. Jan and Jim, Dale and Eileen, Jeff and Jeni, Johnathan, Julie and Mike, Trae, Gabriel and Tiffany, John and Corrie, Sarah, Gus and Sami, Lisa and Brent, on whatever continent we find ourselves together, we are family.

Emma, Evan, Josh, and Aidan, Marlen, Marilin, Olga, Carolina, and Lupita—our family is anything but normal, but I never get tired of sharing our stories. You all stun me continually with how you understand God's movement in your lives and include others in our family. I love coming home to you at the end of each day. I will be relentless in hoping for your stories.

I also want to thank Ray Vanderlaan, unbelievable Bible teacher and Christ follower, who led a life-changing (for me) trip to Israel. Many of the Old Testament illustrations in this book were either drawn from his teaching or came from study I pursued as a result of what I saw and experienced and learned on that trip.

Sweet friends—you know who you are—you have read drafts, prayed on discouraging days, and voted on covers. You have shared your homes, resources, wisdom, and chocolate. Thank you for enriching my life with honest feedback and sincere encouragement. I love the family and fellowship we experience.

Thank you readers, may these stories spur you on to set yourselves in the heavenlies, and believe with ever more conviction that . . . the story isn't over yet.

You who know, O Lord,
Remember me, take notice of me. . . .
Your words were found and I ate them,
And Your words became for me a joy and the delight of my heart;
For I have been called by Your name,
O Lord God of hosts.

. . . . . .

Why has my pain been perpetual
And my wound incurable, refusing to be healed?
Will You indeed be to me like a deceptive stream
With water that is unreliable?

Therefore, thus says the Lord,
"If you return, then I will restore you—
Before Me you will stand;
And if you *extract the precious from the worthless,*
You will become My spokesman.
They for their part may turn to you,
But as for you, you must not turn to them.

"Then I will make you to this people
A fortified wall of bronze;
And though they fight against you,
They will not prevail over you;
For I am with you to save you
And deliver you," declares the Lord.
"So I will deliver you from the hand of the wicked,
And I will redeem you from the grasp of the violent."

—From Jeremiah's prayer and God's response,
Jeremiah 15:15-21 (*NASB*, emphasis added)

HOPE

INTRODUCTION

The buses to the away games, the water bottles we shared, the uniforms. Growing up, I loved playing sports. All year round with the same girls, and our ever-increasing skills. After lost games, I had to pretend to be sadder than I really was. For me it was always more about the camaraderie and less about the season record.

In the fall we played volleyball until our palms were red and our knees bruised. In the winter it was basketball, and I responded to everything about the game, especially how fast it was and how aggressive I could be. Then, come spring, we laced up our running shoes with the boys and played our one co-ed sport—chasing each other around a track until we literally fell over. Still today, I have scars with cinders in them (from the days before asphalt tracks). Finally, June rolled around and it was camps and clinics and summer leagues to stay in shape until the fall.

"You think you can make it?"

My involvement in sports started sometime around my fifth-grade year and continued until eventually I graduated from high school. Despite my best hopes, genetics would determine I stop growing somewhere in the ninth grade. So throughout high school, my 5'4" frame wasn't getting a lot of action under anyone's basket. I learned though, if I wanted to ever play basketball and more importantly, contribute, I needed to learn to develop an outside shot. So for many years

Beth (#42) and her high school basketball team.

I worked on my arc and accuracy until I could be the player people would pass to on the top of the key.

During a basketball tournament in high school over the Christmas holidays, our team was winning each bracket, until eventually we earned a spot in the final game. We played evenly against our competition throughout the entire four quarters, and found ourselves down by one with less than thirty seconds left on the game clock.

Coach Stan Kiehl called a time-out and looked at me. "Do you think if we get you the ball, you could pop one up from the outside before they have a chance to organize much of a defense? You think you can make it?"

I looked around the huddle and said, more confidently than I felt, "Yes, get it to me. I'll do it, Coach."

My friend Dawn dribbled down the court and passed me the ball, where I squared up, eyed the backboard, and threw up the shot.

It ringed around the rim . . . and then rolled out.

Seconds later, the buzzer went off and the game was over. We'd lost the tournament by one point.

I don't remember much about the after-game speech our coach gave; what I most remember was not wanting to face the parents of my friends, who I knew would offer me looks of frustration or pity, or some combination. I took my time gathering my things and finally, when I was sure everyone was gone, I made my way out of the locker room to see who was waiting to take me home.

As I walked through the double doors into the gym, I saw my dad with a ball under his arm. He didn't say anything, just looked me in the eye and bounced me the ball, pointing on the floor to where I had missed the shot. I caught the ball, and feeling frustrated (with him, the game, myself) I squared up and shot.

Swish.

I rolled my eyes and held up two fingers, then reached down for my bag. I gave him *the look* teenage girls have perfected that sarcastically implied, *Satisfied?*

He rebounded my ball, ignored that look, and passed the ball to me again, pointing on the floor where I needed to shoot.

I threw the ball up less accurately and still made the basket.

Catching the rebound, he passed me the ball a third time.

Swish.

This went on for another four or five baskets until my quivering lip finally gave way to the tears that had been hovering.

He rebounded the last ball and cocking his head, looked at me, not with frustration, but with tenderness.

What? I thought, confused. *What is it that you want?*

When he saw my face, he quickly came over and wrapped his arms around me in a bear hug.

Sighing, after a moment he pulled back to look me in the eye, "Honey, I just wanted you to go to bed tonight remembering what it is you are *capable* of."

———————

There are scores of Bible verses I read that implore us to "sit in the heavenly realms" and "fix our eyes on Jesus" and "set our minds on things above," and they are poetic and lyrical and mystical and beautiful. But applicable? What do those words even mean?

How do we live in the midst of this broken world, getting our feet tripped up on all sorts of places, and not look down more than we look up? When we find our story has taken on a dark chapter, either by our own wanderings, or someone else's, do we close our eyes and muddle through? Do we just stay there, now that the consequential scar might stand out, obvious to all? Do we keep our mouths shut until our story has a bow on the end of it and now can be properly considered a "testimony"?

> How do we experience God in the midst of our missed shots?

How do we experience God in the midst of our missed shots? Is it even possible that when he looks at us, he sees only what we are capable of and not the moments when we lose the game?

I had jokingly called this manuscript "conversations in pain without cliché," because it's quite honestly a collection of stories that aren't all easy to read. But they testify to this overarching truth—they put some skin on the often-repeated quotation: "And we know that in all things God works for the good of those who love him, who have been called according to his purpose" (Romans 8:28).

There is a promise he will work on our behalf, despite the circumstances and the other characters in our story—a promise the enemy doesn't get the last word, and the scar we've incurred doesn't define us. It's a promise that whatever we might be experiencing today is just one chapter in a story he is writing and the story isn't over yet. He is extracting the precious truths Jeremiah refers to—precious promises, precious lessons, precious intimacy with him—from the seemingly worthless circumstances, pain, situations, relationships, so that we can be called his spokesmen.

I started this study because I wanted to learn more how to do that. There are far more sticky situations in my day than miraculous moments. I want to hear and see and experience challenges and difficulties and setbacks and not immediately look down or focus on the missed shot, but train my eyes to extract the precious.

And that's key to our contentment. As Christians, we should be marked by our radically different approach to life. We have access to a God who offers us peace, but some days the most conflicted people I talk to are believers. I am a vessel for an unending source of love; however, I can be guilty of wild judgment of those different from me. We have a God depositing into us all manner of wisdom; however, Christians can sound downright ignorant. I want my approach to challenges, to heartbreak, to failure to be a true reflection of my position in Christ. I want to live by the verses I sing in the choruses on Sunday, songs about how I am content, and all I need is Jesus (not Jesus plus the right diagnosis, or Jesus plus having my way).

If I get to be his spokesman, it'll be by reflecting to the world, as the prophet Jeremiah did, a truth not easily understood. And in this case, the truth is, even the most worthless of moments, whether big or small, can have something precious extracted from them. He doesn't waste anything.

Broken marriages, addictions run amuck, pain at the hand of someone least expected, failed pregnancies, failed tests, and failed

> There is nothing worthless, not even a hurricane, that God can't bring something useful or precious out of.

relationships are more the rule than the exception these days, and the world isn't planning on turning itself around anytime soon. Once it does, and we have the perspective of the great cloud of witnesses, we will understand the chapter we are in will one day move into another, and the lessons we have learned as we trained our eyes to seek the truth will be applied to other days. Those days will blend into each other and make up a life story that isn't over until we see the greater purpose on the other side of eternity. Until then, we can just strain our eyes to see something worth redeeming, worth repairing, worth rebuilding . . . and that to me does seem to be the definition of "setting our minds on things above."

Hurricane Alex pummeled my third-world city of Monterrey, Mexico, this week with almost forty inches of rain in as many hours. The city has widespread damage and devastation. Our little ministry campus felt under assault while the rain relentlessly demanded to go where it wanted.

I was outside, in the thick of the storm, bailing out buckets of rainwater alongside a motley crew of visiting guests, long-time staff friends, and some of the orphan teens that live with us. In the middle of it all, I stopped and realized what should have been crushing actually was joyful. We were fearful for our homes and mentally calculating the cost of damage as it was happening, but we were all in this together and were building a certain intimacy as we ganged up together against the storm.

It was in that moment, with dozens of us standing together protecting the property and each other, wearing ponchos that had long since seemed useless, and sleep deprived to the point of being slap-happy, that I realized all over again the truth of Jeremiah's words. There is nothing worthless, not even a hurricane, that God can't bring something useful or precious out of. I could choose to look at the rain, and the mud, and focus on the worthless, or I could look at the deepening connection with friends and the fragile outreach to my neighbors and see the precious.

I hit a turning point around inch twenty, when I realized I was wasting far too much time wondering *Why doesn't he stop it?* Instead, I could have been marveling at a God who allows all of creation the free will to live a life of our own choosing and yet still reaches down and redeems, repairs, restores.

Hurricane Alex has been over now for less than a week. We have to-do lists a mile long as we begin the cleanup process, but I am determined to focus on the good that has and will come out of this storm. The celebration of provision, the delicate new connectedness we feel with some around us who previously had stiff-armed our efforts, the intimacy in our community, the reminder of what is really important—my list of the "precious" is just beginning.

I am promising myself to fix on that precious when it's tempting to look down at the septic water in my kitchen. It feels like exercising a muscle, and I have a choice to learn to pick up what feels heavy and watch it strengthen, or let the heavy things in my life pin me down.

It's more than looking on the bright side of things—which somehow implies that when we grieve a loss or a sin, we are living on the dark side. Extracting the precious isn't about dark or light, it's not about mood or personality, it's about wisdom. It's not an attempt to brush over what is hard or painful, it's an exercise in finding perspective, context, hope.

As you read these stories, you will be entering into firsthand accounts from people who have experienced this kind of exercise. These are stories that, if I were to act as a reporter and check with other witnesses, might contradict another person's view. The facts might look different from the outside. But these stories are the truth for the people who experienced them.

We cannot measure one situation against the other and rank each in value (as if we would or could chose infertility over job loss, or cancer over addiction). These are the consequences of sin (ours and others') and of daily life in a broken world. Being a believer doesn't make us immune from these types of stories; being a believer doesn't mean we get a better version of life to live. But it does guarantee we get to choose a different way of responding, a way that puts those events into a timeline not stuck in the moment, but spanning all of eternity.

I am complicated, a combination of the new self God is making in me and of the flesh I wrestle into submission on my best days. That makes me long to live within God's boundaries. Yet I am a natural-born rule breaker.

I am not in the pew alone. Looking down the aisle, there is far more represented there than the best foot we put forward in fellowship. Every one of has a story. Some have a confession. A few are holding grudges. And most of us harbor a secret. As you read these stories, realize that they represent real people, who lived these real incidents (or still are living them) while they taught your Sunday school class, led your worship, and attended your small group.

Most of them never let on they were struggling. They didn't know they were allowed. But they invite you now to see their missed shots and failed attempts. To exercise relentless hope—standing on your tiptoes, waiting and anticipating God's movement in your story. And believing not only in what he will and can do, but in what he has created you to be capable of.

> *I know that you can do all things,*
> *no purpose of yours can be thwarted.*
>
> —JOB 42:2

I remember everything about *the day*. Anyone with a cancer diagnosis in their family knows what I mean. The day in your life where you can draw a line and know that all events from here on out will be referenced as "before the day" or "after the day."

Our day was August 25, 1995.

I wouldn't have been able to tell you that night, or even still a hundred nights later, that I was in pain. A shot went off at some starting gate—the adrenaline was so strong, I felt more like I was be-

> God would protect us, right? Isn't that what the Bible said?

ginning a race than suffering disappointment. I didn't even know where I was running (toward a happy ending, I am sure), but I know it felt good to be on the move. We were active and fighting an ugly beast I had been certain was never supposed to come to our house. God would protect us, right? Isn't that what the Bible said?

I was wrong on some count, although I wasn't sure which one, and as the beast came, it began to destroy our lives. Or at least it threatened to destroy our lives. It's funny though, when we look back on that year, the memories are unusually intense. They could sound almost pleasant to a third-party observer.

Beth and her dad at her wedding, November 26, 1994.

We stopped all nonessential activity. We cherished time together and planned extraordinarily meaningful family events. We were available to one another in unprecedented ways. We prayed and worshipped and read like our lives depended on it, or at least like my dad's life did.

There are memories of deep emotions and devastating highs and lows.

"The counts are lower!"

"The cancer is spreading."

"The doctor said he was a candidate!"

"The chemo isn't working."

"How do we plan for the future?"

Future?

All the farther I could see was to the end of the day.

It was lunchtime, so I had an hour free without clients at the language/cultural business center where I was working downtown. I should have felt freedom; I normally loved exploring our city on foot, trying new restaurants and meeting friends for an urban afternoon. But this day, I was reeling.

I was known in our family for quoting the story in which Elijah poured water on the altar before he called down the fire, so that when the fire came, it would be even more miraculous. The grimmer the prognosis, the more convinced I would become that God was only upping the ante.

But a large bucket of water had come the night before in the form of more bad news, and instead of feeling anticipatory, I just felt . . . wet.

I have always loved the Old Testament; its stories captivate me. They inspire me with the idea that ordinary people can live extraordinary lives. In those stories are my childhood versions of superheroes: Esther, who faced the king; David, who slew Goliath; Joshua, whose unusual battle techniques made him famous. I ate my lunch salad in silence in my office, thinking about these heroes of old. Did they ever feel wet like I did?

I pulled out my laptop and, propping my feet up on my desk, I leaned back and tried to imagine what God would say to some of my favorite characters. How would he encourage them? Would it sound like encouragement to me? We have the hindsight in their stories they weren't privy to—I know Esther saved her people, and the giant went down with a stone, and the walls fell down. There was no hindsight in my story yet. I still didn't know whether my dad would die or survive. What were they feeling in the midst of their stories? Could I relate?

My hand flew over the keys as I pictured myself listening in on their prayers and God's responses back to them. It was such a relief to think about someone else's problems for that hour, and those Old Testament characters had some serious ones: infertility, imprisonment, unwanted pregnancy, wayward children. I started to wonder—would it have seemed to them like God was silent in those circumstances, when in reality, he was probably talking louder than ever before? I wrote my dad a letter with all the thoughts I had, hoping to encourage both him and myself that the God he had taught me about would save the day, one way or another.

I didn't want to admit it at the time, but as I look back now, I realize I was still clinging to a childish faith, one where the score was always settled in my favor and God always came through (how I asked him to). I had a strong faith in God, but I had fashioned God into something he wasn't. I now reference that time as my "genie God" days. I hoped by rubbing his belly, I could produce a God who would grant my wishes.

> I had fashioned God into something he wasn't.

Of course, I never said it like that. I said that all things would work out if I prayed where two or three were gathered, or if I prayed with holy oil, or if I, as a resident of God's kingdom on earth, prayed and rejected the illness. Doesn't matter how I said it, what I meant was, "God, if you really love us, you will stop this." What I didn't say, but equally meant was, "And if you don't, I am not sure I can believe in you."

So to whom will you compare me, the Incomparable?
Can you picture me without reducing me?
People with a lot of money
hire craftsmen to make them gods.
The artisan delivers the god,
and they kneel and worship it!
They carry it around in holy parades,
then take it home and put it on a shelf.
And there it sits, day in and day out,
a dependable god, always right where you put it.
Say anything you want to it, it never talks back.
Of course, it never does anything either!
Think about this. Wrap your minds around it.

This is serious business, rebels. Take it to heart.
Remember your history,
your long and rich history.
I am God, the only God you've had or ever will have—
incomparable, irreplaceable—
From the very beginning
telling you what the ending will be,
All along letting you in
on what is going to happen,
Assuring you, "I'm in this for the long haul,
I'll do exactly what I set out to do," . . .
I've said it, and I'll most certainly do it.
I've planned it, so it's as good as done.
(Isaiah 46:5-11, *The Message*)

As the year wore on, he only got sicker. But I still knew my God would save the day; he always did. I thought my dad knew that as well, so I was surprised when he began to prepare me for his death. I didn't want to hear any of it, and changed the subject abruptly with each attempt. Now as a parent, I realize you are never without opportunity for influence, and he was trying his hardest to use his final days to convince me this was not a situation without hope. And hope could maybe be in something higher than a clean bill of health.

That last week of his life, a relative called him from out of town. He urged her to come right then while he could still see her, instead of traveling for the funeral. It was a Monday afternoon when she arrived, and I excused myself from the room so they could have some time alone. After about an hour she left, and I could see her

HIS STORY ISN'T OVER

My friend J.J. has been struggling this year with a significant (is there any other kind?) tumor in his jaw. I asked him to sum up his experience.

"'You have cancer, and it's serious.' That's how it started. I have had some doubts and questions for God in the midst of this difficult process. I felt confronted with the question, Will I trust God or not in this? I'm remembering God is the same yesterday, today, and tomorrow and he loves me and promises to never leave me. In Philippians 4:12, Paul wrote 'I have learned the secret of being content in any and every situation.' God is enough for me, and I'm moving toward Paul's attitude in Philippians 1:21: 'For to me, to live is Christ and to die is gain.' May he be glorified now and always."

eyes were red from crying. I walked into the hospital room, expecting to see him wiped out from that long exchange, and instead he was sitting up and animated. "Beth, it will all be worth it if she comes to the kingdom with us." He looked at me, willing me to understand.

#$%@#? All worth it? What planet was he living on? I could think of no circumstance that would make the last year "worth it."

I wish I had known then he was modeling for me the practice of extracting the precious from the worthless. It would have made that exchange all the more sweet, and I might have even joined him. But he (whose mind was set on things above) was the only one between the two of us who could see the higher value of her salvation.

Just a week later, we all gathered around his bed for his last night with us. I was holding on to more than his hand. I was holding on to pretense—an agreement I had made along the way that if all my stories didn't end as I wished them, then God had somehow failed me. It was an untruth, and like he does to his children who are suffering, he extended me an additional grace, to manage what I couldn't with my own resources. To take what I realize now resembled more like a mustard seed of real faith and make it still be enough. I felt that deposit of grace as Dad slipped from us.

"Absent from the body means present with the Lord." My mom whispered Paul's words from 2 Corinthians to us as her husband breathed his final breath. And then suddenly, eternity for me had an address. It became a place instead of a concept. It was real, and my dad, among many others, now lived there.

> I could think of no circumstance that would make the last year "worth it."

Truthfully, my grieving wasn't very pretty. I had all the normal stages, including anger. But my childish faith died in Christ Hospital next to his earthly body, and in its place was born something of a faith that was, particularly now, mine. It was dynamic (not plastic or pretty) and willing to be stretched. I learned my God could handle my questions and my doubts, because he was unchanging and perfect and wholly sure of himself. I've counted on that in the last decade and a half, because I have grown to appreciate his patience with my questions, almost as much as the perfectness of his answers. He is looking at our whole lives at one time; he doesn't live it linearly with us. He saw my dad from birth to death to rebirth again, and he created him for eternity. That plan, that story, wasn't thwarted by multiple myeloma.

I think we cannot help as we grow but to store our faith in a frame. When God operates outside of what we can understand or can explain away, we are faced with two choices. To dismiss that action as either false or unloving, or to grow our frame and thus our understanding of what he is capable. I had to ask myself in this season: Was I willing to grow my faith to the point that I believed there is no circumstance that he can't use for his glory and our greater good? Or would I keep my faith inside a frame I had always known and diminish what could come of such a terrible reality?

I had made God into something he was not, like a personal magician whom I could coax into doing a trick for me. Today, fifteen-plus years wiser and vastly more exposed to needs that are painful and circumstances not easily solved, I believe in a bigger God. I believe in a God who has our whole lives in his hands, and whose timing is clearly different than mine. Could God be more than a chronological order of days—could his story have started long before I arrived and still be going on after its perceived end?

> Was I willing to grow my faith to the point that I believed there is no circumstance that he can't use for his glory and our greater good?

The story of Dad's illness and subsequent death still isn't over yet, no matter how much it felt like the end when it happened. I could try to explain his death with layers of stories that came in the season following the funeral, but that doesn't feel right. I know God could have touched those lives in lots of ways without killing off my dad to do it.

I think rather that we live in a world that has been broken, broken physically and spiritually. God could have pulled his hands off and watched it all spiral out of control with sin, disease, pain, and war. Instead, he has chosen to intervene, to redeem what is happening and to use situations, all situations, regardless of their causes, for his greater good and the good of those bearing witness to it. He has made us to be in relationship with him, and for that relationship to be evolving/growing as we experience the life and faith around us.

I wish I could have learned this lesson and experienced that intimacy in a million other ways, but one thing I get to take away from Dad's death is, when I intersect with a situation, a circumstance, a relationship and I find it too hard/big/difficult/heavy to lift, I remind myself I am looking at it from one point in time. And there are plotlines going on all around that point that will culminate in the next chapter.

The story isn't over yet. The frame can be expanded, and it won't break.

HER STORY ISN'T OVER

SEE how the older girl's mouth is open as she feeds her little sister? I love this picture—it reflects the love and concern of an older sibling. So often the oldest child in an orphaned sibling group is asked of far more than they developmentally should provide: problem solving, bartering for shelter or food, protecting the younger children from abuses—all at their own expense. Then, if and when they should ever become available for adoption, it's the oldest child who is often passed over, even after years of sacrifice.

PERSPECTIVE

I was speaking at a missionary gathering in Nigeria: some seventy women had come together that evening for much more than what this speaker could offer. They were there to remember they weren't alone. That there are others who live their same strange lives, making a way in a culture not their own, sacrificing their comfort untold times a day for a reward they believe is still ahead. Strong women.

Each had her own ministry specialty. Some were translators—working most of the time in the bush, hammering out one of the country's 250 tribal languages into Scripture. Others worked in churches or schools, film evangelism or orphan care. And one woman I spoke with had a ministry in the brothels.

Intrigued, I asked her some questions about it. Statistics vary, but some claim as high as ninety percent of orphans worldwide go into the black market or prostitution, so I was drawn to hear some of her stories. A few of them later, I commented to her how impressed I was with her perspective on such hard work.

> Like two sides of a single coin, faith and hope when rooted in love make a spirit virtually unbreakable.

"My perspective?" she laughed. "I was inspired to move here during a short-term visit when someone took me to an old missionary cemetery here in the country. I knew God was calling our family to something, but I was struggling at what cost a move here would require. Then I heard the stories of these missionaries from 200 years ago. Man, my perspective is nothing compared to theirs."

Perplexed, I tilted my head, inviting the lesson I imagined was to come.

"Their life expectancy once landing in Africa was about three to five years. Many died of disease, others were martyred, some died in conflicts. . . . Knowing this was their fate, they packed their belongings in coffins before they shipped them over. Their families and churches, in lieu of going-away parties, would host funerals for them, so that all could say their proper good-byes. Once they left home, they were essentially marching to their deaths, with the hope of bringing as much life to this continent as possible on their way out."

My mouth hung open, and one phrase flashed through my mind.

Relentless hope.

This was a testimony of a different kind of hope. I recognize it now when I see it; it is relentless in its nature and added to it is a faith in a God who sees it all. Like two sides of a single coin, faith and hope when rooted in love make a spirit virtually unbreakable. These pioneer missionaries were setting out to a huge unknown, believing in a call they had from someone they had never seen. They had hope in a country with little fruit. Hope in a future generation who would need to continue the cause. Hope in an eternal reward, waiting for them. Not casual hope, not hope when it's convenient, but a relentless, barreling-toward-it, life-changing, deal-breaking hope.

2

GOING AFTER THE ONE

Count on it—there's more joy in heaven over one sinner's rescued life than over ninety-nine good people in no need of rescue.
—LUKE 15:7 (*THE MESSAGE*)

The call came one afternoon from a Mexican government social worker who oversees an overcrowded orphanage with the toughest cases. A sea of lost children clinging to lost children, hurt people, hurting people—a truly dismal surrounding for even the strongest soul.

"We have two case files we would like you to consider for your teen program . . . " she started out, all business. Our ministry cares for orphans in the third world, and in Mexico, we take orphans aging out of the system and put them through higher education, where they live among our staff and are discipled as they join our families.

I listened for a moment, and then interjected, "I am sorry, we only take children from private, faith-based institutions. I am afraid we won't be able to accommodate these students." I prepared to hang up.

She offered in staccato, "Two sisters. Only been here a short while. Please."

I said, regretfully, "Thanks for the call."

And hung up.

Two days later as the phone rang in my hand, I turned it over to see the same number on my caller ID. I decided avoidance would just breed persistence on her part, so I answered.

"I was hoping to have someone bring over their case file for you to read," she started off, not even introducing herself this time.

"It's nothing against your students, honestly; it's just a door we don't want to open. You could fill our limited spots up in a day with students who've had a wealth of difficult circumstances. We place children in families, and we have no experience to know if your students would be able to adapt to all we would be asking of them. I'm sorry, I know that sounds harsh; it's just the truth."

Siblings offer shelter to each other.

She paused, as if she were a recording, then proceeded, "OK, so I will make an extra copy of the file, and have it couriered to you this afternoon. If after reading it you aren't interested, I will leave you alone."

I hung up. It felt like I lost that round.

We received the file on the two girls the next day and after reading it, and praying, Todd and Matt (another staff member) decided to meet these sisters.

I humbly called back my new friend. "We will come over to your government compound and meet the girls later this week, but I warn you, don't tell them about us. I don't want them getting hurt if we end up not feeling like it's a good fit."

The next afternoon, there was a knock at our door; the social worker had dropped by with the girls. The interview turned into an invitation for the weekend. That afternoon, as they spilled their story out to us, I was dumbstruck. Their mother died of disease the year before, leaving them in the hands of a stepfather who had for years already been abusing them. Without the slight protection their mother offered, the abuse grew in frequency and fierceness. Complicating matters, he was a member of the police force and threatened severe consequences if they ever told anyone.

One day, the eldest sister snapped and finally told a friend's father, who drove them directly to the government orphanage and social work center.

There the girls recounted their story. When they were finished, the social worker explained the volatile atmosphere of the orphanage, and that in some ways they would be trading one hell for another.

"Nothing is as bad as what we have experienced this year," said the oldest sister, and the girls checked into the orphanage of their own will.

THEIR STORY ISN'T OVER

ACCORDING to UNICEF, there are an estimated 30 million orphans in India alone. The girls pictured here are just a sampling. They live in a safe place, but millions of their counterparts are subject to exploitation, and at risk to be enslaved. Every 2.2 seconds, another orphan "ages out" of a system, without a place to go or a plan. Our response can be multi-layered. Some are called to go, some are called to adopt, some are called to pray, some are called to mentor, some are called to give, some are called to speak for them, and others are called to serve. It's not a question of whether or not to go after the "one," but how and when and where.

> *Then Jesus told them this parable: "Suppose one of you has a hundred sheep and loses one of them. Doesn't he leave the ninety-nine in the open country and go after the lost sheep until he finds it? And when he finds it, he joyfully puts it on his shoulders and goes home. Then he calls his friends and neighbors together and says, 'Rejoice with me; I have found my lost sheep.'"* (Luke 15:3-6)

Lately, I have been fascinated with this parable. I am in awe of a God who doesn't look at the ninety-nine and think he has pretty good odds. I often erroneously attribute human tendencies to God (like fatigue, or irritation, or in this case, mediocrity), and so I am amazed that he doesn't just stick around in the midst of those ninety-nine and enjoy their fellowship. It's what I am tempted to do most days.

> Our churches have pews full of people who are tired of G-rated stories only being told with glossy, happy endings.

Instead, this God has an eye that has never left the "one," that sees wherever it has scampered off to, either out of rebellion or in escape. He understands its story with its complexity and in its entirety, and still is without judgment.

There has been a moment in every believer's life when we were that sheep around his shoulders; when he caught up with us and brought us home. What happens then? Well, when we spend time around the other ninety-nine, there can be friction. At its best, the good kind of friction we label as accountability. At its worst, it creates conflict and divides families, churches, friendships, marriages, and countries, and can cause even found sheep to wish they were lost again.

That weekend those girls landed in the middle of a ministry campus where they suddenly had a whole host of adults concerned about their well-being. They didn't understand who Christ was when they arrived, but now, years later, they know of his love. He saw them being mistreated, he saw them in pain, and he led them to our path because he is writing a story just for them and wanted to use this body to represent his body. He is interrupting what should be the expected next events of their story to redirect its path.

It's what he does, he comes in.

And as they are rebuilding their lives and their trust in people and their faith in him, he continues doing what he does, giving them strength, grace, vision—using their past to give them resolve and empathy and a whole other host of qualities that haven't yet been born. Instead of asking "Where was he when it was happening?" or "How can I love a God who let that happen to me?", the girls are learning to worship a God who never gave up his pursuit of them and who will use even the most painful parts of their journey for their future good.

ONE LOST SHEEP

Our churches have pews full of people who are tired of the party of the ninety-nine with smiles painted on and G-rated stories only being told with glossy, happy endings. Instead we long to share what storms we have been through, to find encouragement in authentic—no more labels or excuses, no more posing—kind of fellowship most of us sheep truly long for. We want to talk about the pain chapters and together celebrate the precious we've extracted.

When I first met the lady whose story I recount here, my first impression was her strength. I don't know why it never occurred to me until recently that we only get strong muscles when we work out, so why would we suddenly get an inner strength without a challenge?

I asked her what chapter in her story was the seed to her strength and she told me what follows. This is just one family's story. It can never be repeated, not the pattern, nor the solution, because each family is unique. But as I listened to this mother pour out her story to me, I was reminded powerfully of this singular truth: there is no one chasing after our children like the Shepherd.

———————

"Our son was such a sweetie growing up, tenderhearted and very funny. He was always extremely engaging, holding the whole room captivated. It worked in his favor while making friends, which was helpful since we moved every several years. Even later, in the midst of his rebellion, he still had a sparkle in his eye." She paused, and I could tell her mind's eye was seeing him as a child.

I waited, thinking, *Let her enjoy this memory.*

She started up again, "He was always smaller, the youngest in his class. I suppose it was a mistake, but I allowed him to start school very young. When we moved, he always seemed to find new friends. It wasn't a problem for him until he reached junior high. It was the end of seventh grade and we moved him mid-year to Chicago; that's the first time I noticed an attitude. I would wonder if what I was seeing was just his personality; it seemed normal, definitely manageable."

Every young boy gets angry with his sisters, right?

"We learned later, he was getting a lot of teasing at school, being called 'the runt.' He would come home and bring that pent-up frustration with him. Then we moved again to Indianapolis and he had to find another set of new friends, and as a ninth grader it was much harder. His saving grace was his musical talent, and so his new friends came from the band.

"When he joined the jazz band, I was thrilled. The kids seemed nice, his grades were excellent, and I had no idea some of these new friends were considered 'party animals.' By his junior year, his attitude had grown considerably worse and he would talk disrespectfully to me. Now he listened exclusively to heavy metal bands.

"He was old enough to get a job and with his new money, he bought a car. The worst thing we had to deal with was a few speeding tickets, which we made him pay with his own savings. At this point, we were still chalking it up to life experiences and poor choices. I know now he was already drinking, but then I didn't fully realize it. I couldn't imagine what he was rebelling against; I don't remember ever comparing him to our other children.

"I couldn't imagine what he was rebelling against."

"When we recognized he had a problem with social drinking, we placed some restrictions on him, and we certainly thought we were addressing it. We prayed all the time, and would lie in bed and think of ways we could compliment him on something, anything, so we'd zero in on his great sense of humor.

"We wanted to help him feel good about himself, so he wouldn't resort to this behavior. We decided to pick and choose our battles, and allow him to grow out his hair, even though we prefer it short.

"We were mainly praying at this stage, but not feeling panicky."

Then came homecoming weekend.

"The band was going to be playing at the football game. We almost always went to the games, but this one night we couldn't. Later we

OUR STORY ISN'T OVER

"WE have this hope as an anchor for the soul, firm and secure. It enters the inner sanctuary behind the curtain, where our forerunner, Jesus, has entered on our behalf" (Hebrews 6:19, 20). Hope isn't something we have to muster up, it's not a practice or a discipline; it's a gift. This chapter in Hebrews addresses God's long history of covenant-keeping and the hope we can experience as a result. He has never let go.

received a phone call from our local hospital—our son was getting his stomach pumped because he was drunk, in danger of alcohol poisoning. We prayed all the way to the ER. They released him, but since he was acting out his drunkenness on school grounds, he was suspended. In the top ten percent of his class, this really messed up his grades to be out for a couple of weeks. The school placed two conditions on his return: he had to make up his grades and he had to receive counseling. A counselor was chosen and he followed the directives given, and for a season, things seemed better.

"The following year, we were cautiously optimistic. I was focusing on the fact he had been accepted to his first choice of colleges; he had a job and things seemed almost normal for a change. And then the police called the house to report he had been arrested for stealing from the store where he worked after school. Up until now, we had always been giving him the benefit of the doubt. But that afternoon, it all changed. He was stealing and he used a friend as an accomplice! At only seventeen years of age, thankfully he was not yet considered an adult. At his court trial, the judge determined his record could be wiped clean if he completed community service and stayed out of trouble.

"At this point, I was feeling I needed to know everything, so I started going through his dresser, his closet, and I found more evidence he had wandered far from his Christian roots. We were still communicating, but we seldom saw him; he was now spending more time with his friends than with the family.

"The next year, he headed off to college, and ran up a credit card debt totaling $4000. It was further evidence his life was out of control. We weren't seeing a lot of him, but in a way that broke my heart, it was better. When he was in the house, there was tension and everything became a battle. He talked back to me, exerting independence he hadn't earned. One dark evening in our story, my son spoke to me very disrespectfully. My husband, hearing him, ran into the room quick as a jackrabbit, grabbed him by the collar, and pushed him up against the wall, his voice escalating, 'You will NEVER talk to your mother that way!' Neither my son nor I had ever seen him lose his temper before.

"I knew we were in a whole new world.

"As I share what happens next in our story, let me start with saying we were at a breaking point. And we believed in the principle of tough love. So we prayed and talked and cried and prayed again until we felt a peace about asking our son to leave our home. We didn't want him influencing our youngest child still living with us; we didn't want him bringing his attitude and tension to our dinner table. We asked him to pack his suitcases and told him (in love), 'Get on with your life, have at it, do it your own way, kid.'

"Sometimes he would call, but many days passed without contact. The relief in the house was palpable. Not in our hearts—those were always heavy—but in the house for sure.

"I remember at one point in this season, we received a phone call from the police, saying our son was in their 'drunk tank.' They asked what we wanted to do, and we chose not to bail him out. Lying in bed, we pleaded with the Lord, 'Take him as low as he has to go, and bring him where he needs to be, but please, don't let him die.'

"As a mother, I worried more, probably cried more, but I was in total agreement with my husband: tough love was what our son needed."

———————————

However, they did let him come home. When he flunked out of college, he returned to the house, but only under their conditions. During the next six months, his life didn't really change, but he seemed to be able to hold down a job. Still, free nights were spent partying.

She went on, "Then God in his wisdom moved us to North Carolina. It sure didn't seem like wisdom at the time, and leaving him behind was hard. But now we look back and see our son still had farther to fall. Once we moved, he was forced to bunk again with friends. He was twenty-three years old and he didn't know where he was going, or really who he was. We hoped and prayed with each interaction that he was getting closer to realizing his way was not working.

"Finally, a breakthrough came on Christmas Eve. We were apart on this holiday—several states apart—and I was thinking about where he was, who he would be with on this special day. We were getting ready to leave for church when the phone rang.

"'Dad, pray for me.' Then he hung up.

"We knew he was troubled, as his lifeline was now gone. We were gone. There were no more meals, no more hugs. I knew he had been heading toward a crash for a while, and in a way it would be a relief to get there, but I was suddenly nervous. 'Did it sound like he was going to commit suicide?' I asked my husband, voice shaking.

"We simply looked at each other, nodded, and then bowed to pray. Moments later, the phone rang again.

"'Please tell Mom I am not going to commit suicide.' And he hung up. Recalling that memory today, it's almost comical how well he knew what I was thinking, but back then there was only a wash of instant relief.

> "He was twenty-three years old and he didn't know where he was going, or really who he was."

"We called his siblings and some of our praying friends. We asked them to engage in prayer for him like they hadn't ever before.

"Our daughter was only one state away, getting ready to celebrate her first Christmas with her fiancé and his family when we reached her. Her response was instant. 'We'll go. We can leave right now, Mom. It will take us two hours or so to get there, but if he's calling out for help, we have to respond.'

"I still don't know all that happened that night. I've been told that, when they arrived, they went grocery shopping and my daughter made him one of our family dishes for dinner. My guess is they just sat around a lot and were together.

"He says they just loved him, loved on him.

"And it was the moment it counted the most."

———————

Then, sometime in the next couple of months, he picked up a book they had sent him for Christmas: *Tender Warrior* by Stu Weber. That led to a church visit with a friend. And it was during that season that he accepted Christ as his Lord and Savior and truly came home.

She continued, "He tells us almost as soon as he gave his heart to Christ, the desire for chemical dependency disappeared. That same year, the Lord brought his wife into his life, and now he is a loving husband with a houseful of my happy grandchildren. He has worked in youth ministry for many years, and has shared his story with students who can relate to the trials he experienced. He says it's for a reason *testimony* starts with the word *test*. (Although sometimes it can feel like *I* took the test!)

"God will deal with them; it is he who does the chipping, the shaping, the molding."

"Typically, as you get older, you get more narrow-minded. But I am a different person as a result of our long journey with our son. I realize everyone has a story and so as a result, I am less judgmental. Our son's story involved alcohol and drugs; someone else has another story. Living through what we did for those years developed in me a distinct empathy. I used to get so disappointed in people, but I now realize God will deal with them; it is he who does the chipping, the shaping, the molding. My role is to pray, speak the truth in love, and then continue to pray some more.

"The lessons from this season are pouring over me as I relive it here with you. There is so much 'precious' adding up: I believe more in the sovereignty of God and power of prayer than ever before. I will walk forevermore believing it's God who is in control, and I am not to worry. I was a worrier. When my son would break curfew, I would make my husband call the hospitals, fearing always the worst. But I know today, worry is sin. When he would come in (late, but safe), and my worry would turn to anger (which was born in fear), I would lash out with words I didn't mean. That anger would be gasoline on an already well-lit fire, and I would hurt the situation instead of help it. I have since learned how important it is to communicate my fear first, so the person I love hears only my concern.

"We watch our son parent his children today and we are so proud of the man he has become. I see the heart again I nurtured as a child, and I can enjoy the fun he creates wherever he is. The truth is, his family, his testimony, his life—it captivates me."

She stopped talking and I sat quietly, humbled by her honesty and her strength. I asked her if I could pray, for her and her son. She just nodded and I wondered briefly how many times she has bowed with his name on her mind. I began, "Thank you, Father, for the pursuit you led for this one . . . lend us your vision and perspective on lives not yet surrendered to you. Give us wisdom, patience, discernment, hope, peace, and grace in abundance."

3

The LORD will fight for you; you need only to be still.

—EXODUS 14:14

I was with a visiting friend the other day in a really poor neighborhood here in Mexico. Standing on the edge of a small river, we noticed a thin pipe running across the top of opposite banks bringing water from the "civilized" side of the river to the other, where the villagers live without running water. What caught our attention was a line of chickens crossing the river like tightrope walkers, clutching the pipe with their talons. Step over step they balanced top-heavy bodies, painstakingly making their way across the pipe.

We stood there, mesmerized. It kind of looked to me like a *Far Side* cartoon.

Finally my friend broke the silence. "Aren't chickens . . . birds?" he asked, hesitating over each word.

"I sure think so," I casually answered back, not breaking my stare.

"Then . . . don't they have . . . wings?"

"I guess so; I like to eat chicken wings." I smiled, knowing where he was headed.

He then dove into the river and started clapping and yelling underneath the birds, trying to scare them off the pole. They began to protest and then unhappily flapped their tiny wings and

virtually sailed across the remaining pipe.

"Yahoo!" He came climbing back up on the bank, triumphantly flinging himself down. "Although painful for sure, we did them a favor. They never have to step carefully again. They now know they are flyers. They can come across at their leisure, whenever they want."

We sat in the dirt—tired from all the excitement, proud.

Several moments of silence passed before our philosophical discussion began. What pipes do we hold on to, when we have wings to fly? What makes someone cling to what seems secure, but is clearly a harder route to cross? What kinds of things scare us enough to let go and use our wings? Do we hold on because everyone else does? Would we be the first to let go, or the last? Do they resent the one who scared them off, or are they now grateful?

The questions kept coming.

We walked down the road for the next hour, visiting families in a neighborhood outreach, praying with them about troubles I have grown used to seeing, but not callous to hearing. Between each house and visit though, we returned to our chicken conversation. It made me giggle, but the metaphors were fascinating.

When it was time to go back to the river, I asked around for a camera. I wanted a picture of the flying chickens.

But when we reached the bank, my heart sank.

Walking again across the tiniest pipe you have ever seen was our same family of poultry.

"Is that why we call someone a bird brain? Did they really already forget?" I asked, frustrated.

My deep-thinking friend shook his head. "Aren't we just the same though? Bursts of glory when we let go, then a return to the same old familiar pattern?"

"Not me. No." I shook my head decidedly. "I want to use my wings. I want to be done with careful walking."

He smiled at me.

"Beth, then it's time to let yourself be shooed off the pipe."

———

When I first started spending time with Jill and heard her story, I would see this chicken story in my mind's eye. It just seemed to me as if she for the first time had found her wings. There were a whole host of people telling her she needed to get back on the pipe—it's where she belonged, it's her label. She's a chicken. But Jill is no chicken, and the more she enjoys flying, the more she is inspiring others to follow.

> What pipes do we hold on to, when we have wings to fly?

Jill showed up today at my home with a mission, a purpose she repeated several times before we began: "I will share this story, not so someone can hear details of my life I would rather leave private. I will share this story, because I think if I had heard something like this earlier, this chapter wouldn't have gone on for as long as it did." Her voice caught and her big eyes filled up with tears.

I sat there quietly, knowing the memories we were stirring up were far from easy.

Settling in, she began, "I grew up in a Christian home, where my mom especially made sure I knew about Jesus. I remember how happy she was when as a five-year-old, I prayed to receive Jesus in my heart. I was happy because she was. I learned as I grew that my faith came with a set of rules—things you were supposed to do, and definitely things you weren't. I was determined to learn the rules and follow them.

"By the time I was in high school, I had found a niche in both sports and music and was happy with how well I performed in these areas. I was growing in my walk with the Lord, and my heart longed to serve others. I loved all the opportunities I had through school and church to exercise my faith.

"Wait a minute, did that just happen?"

"During this time, my older brother and sister were regularly causing my parents trouble with their poor choices and complicated lives, and it felt good to be the child who made everyone happy. This season was punctuated with police visits for my siblings' missteps, and fights between my parents that eventually led to their divorce. I was more determined than ever to not add stress to our family life.

"At sixteen, I had a hard time finding a regular job I could fit around my after-school activities, so it was natural for me to turn to a family friend with his own business, who could offer flexible hours. Through this job, I met the manager, Max, who was more than twice my age. My first impression of him was he was an incredible husband and father; I loved watching him with his wife and kids when they came in. I liked instantly how we connected over our shared faith and love for sports. I trusted him and liked his attention.

"When I look back now and tell you about this first incident, I wonder why I couldn't see the problems coming. In hindsight, it seems so clear, but that first night, I didn't trust myself to read the situation accurately.

"He walked me out to my car after a night of work, then reached out to hug me good-bye. He was between me and the front car door, and then he spun us around and I was pinned against the car, as he turned the hug into more of a body embrace, and leaned hard into me.

"My heart was beating really fast, and I didn't say anything as I got into the car. I was thinking over and over, *What just happened? Wait a minute, did that just happen? No way. What if I am reading into this too much? I can't tell anyone—how embarrassing if he didn't mean anything and I accuse him of it! I mean, he is a Christian. What do I do?*

"If I questioned his intention then, all doubt was erased when he later made more overt inappropriate advances toward me. I remember thinking, *This is very real. Why is he doing this? I thought he cared about me?* I was scared. I was sad. I was frozen.

"I don't expect the average person to understand this, but I am not sharing this, Beth, for the average person, I am sharing it for the reader who knows exactly what I am talking about. I had a voice, but I didn't know how to use it. I was still in high school; I thought no one would believe me. I thought for sure everyone would think I was a bad person. I wanted to say, 'Get away!' I didn't like it at all, but I was so concerned with what others would think. What would my friends think, what would my parents think? Would this ruin my chances to do the things I wanted to in the future?

"I dug a mental hole for myself and I realize now all that thinking just made me more stuck. That's the best way to describe this period, I felt stuck. He always pretended later, in front of others, like nothing happened. I wanted to believe it was nothing, but everything inside of me was screaming otherwise. I didn't want to tell my parents, I didn't want to be one more struggle for them. Everything else was going well, and I didn't want to mess it up. Could I keep it all separate and let my life go on as normal?

"I believed a set of lies about myself and they were daily compounding. Over and over in my head I was repeating, *My life is over. There is no going back from here. I am just going to have to live with this. I can't go back to ever being normal. I am ruined. I feel so defeated. No one will believe me.*

"Then something wonderfully awful happened—an adult found out, two actually. Female friends of his had some suspicions when they saw us interacting, and confronted him. I was so relieved, even though I was worried they would find and then tell my parents. But it turned horribly sour, as the women never talked to his wife, or my mom—the two people I was most terrified would find out, but who I knew had the power to stop it. All it did was reinforce the lies. Max became more aggressive after this, almost empowered. 'You want this,' he said. 'You are responsible.'

"I couldn't tell anyone; I was sure everyone would hate me. I made a contingency plan: if I get pregnant, I am going to have to run away.

"I stopped recognizing myself, as I learned to be an expert liar. I lied to my mom, to my friends, to him, and to myself. One lie spilled into another until I didn't remember the truth; the lying dulled my conviction and had long drowned out any voice of God in my life.

"Normal opportunities came up, and my heart longed to have the freedoms I saw my other friends enjoy. He said no to each one:

'If you go, I am telling everybody about this. They will hate you.'

"This stage was full of threats. At this point, he was utterly controlling me. I now knew his family and he mine. We had hoards of mutual friends.

"I have a thousand little stories from this long season. Stories that can make the bile rise up in my throat. Stories that now, years later, sound like they belong to someone else.

"Most days I woke up with a panicky feeling and I fell asleep with my heart racing. I knew something was going to break inside of me and I was in a full-blown crisis. After three years, I either needed to stand up to him or I was going to admit myself to a hospital—I honestly thought with increasing alarm, *I am going to go insane.*

"Then one Sunday, after church, I decided, 'Today is the day. I am going to do it.'

"I had imagined a million times before what I would say, but I had never been this serious. If my biggest fear was friends and family finding out, Max's was getting caught—both by the law and the Lord. He worried that God would never forgive him. I decided to use that against him.

HER STORY ISN'T OVER

"By his light I walked through darkness" (Job 29:3). This image was taken above the home of the girl who told me this: "My childhood was moving along fine, until my mom died and then we all fell into a deep pit. My sister had to take care of us, even though she was a child herself. Eventually, I spent some time in a government orphanage until I landed here, in a home with Christians. They have taught me God uses everything in my life for a reason and he will continue to be beside me. It was that message that brought me out of the pit."

"So while I had the resolve, I drove over to his house, knowing he was alone. I told him to get away from me—that this had to stop. I lied to him and told him that I had had a dream where I saw he was going to Hell. He literally fell to his knees and panicked. He was sobbing, begging me not to go. He wasn't angry, there were no threats—just a 'You can't do this, you cannot do this.'

"But I did, and I left there—shaking, crying. *Thank God. I did it! I am going to be free! I can live my life!* I was so, momentarily, relieved.

"In the aftermath however, things got much worse. They went from a storm to a tsunami. He would call me dozens of times within a span of fifteen minutes. His friends were calling me, he was threatening he was going to tell my parents. I was still foolishly hoping no one would ever have to know.

"I walked into my house soon thereafter and saw my mom at the table, crying. I looked in her eyes and felt it: *She knows*. Max's wife had told her. I knew she was going to be emotional, and she was. It was the worst timing for her. One of the biggest reasons it went on for so long was so I could avoid this very scene, I was afraid it would put her in her grave—that her heart would literally stop beating. I wasn't excited at this point that she knew, but I was glad it was over. I still thought it was all my fault. I felt shame, guilt, defeat, panic, anxiety. The lie was deafening at this point, 'Everyone is going to hate you.'

"I was exhausted from living an empty life."

"Then God threw me a lifeline, a temporary way out. An out-of-town friend called, unaware of the events unfolding in my life, and invited me to spend the summer away. One of those opportunities normal kids have was suddenly available for me, and I was free to take it. I remember being surprised that God even cared, and it was a relief to think that he did.

"Just because I was free from Max did not mean things automatically got better. That whole first year was hard. Everyone was finding out; I had to recount my version over and over. Rumors were being spread, stories were getting twisted, and I was feeling like I couldn't go anywhere because, who knew? What were they thinking? What would they ask me?

"At first God was the only thing I could hold onto to get through each day. All the shame and embarrassment consumed me and I was praying to a powerful God, asking for a quick healing. I wanted to feel like a normal person again. I was grasping for the God I had grown up learning about, but it wasn't in a relationship kind of way. It was more formulaic and it wasn't very satisfying.

"After a while I got tired of not hearing any answers and thought, *What's the point?* The anger stage followed and lasted for a good six months. I was consumed with a slew of emotions—anger, depression, and bitterness, toward God and Max.

"I had flashbacks and nightmares that kept me up at night, constant fears of running into him. These thoughts controlled the majority of my days. I was in counseling and trying to see how a God I had loved and had loved me could let this happen. I came up with a list of the ways I had seen God. It included: I didn't get pregnant or contract an STD, I have some friends and mentors who want to support and encourage me, I never took my own life, I have the chance to still study, and he gave me the strength to eventually get out.

"I wanted to start listening to God. I was tired of being angry. It gets so heavy carrying around all of that bitterness and anger. Still today, I have good days and bad days but the good ones are now outweighing the bad. My young cousin died this year and her death made me question how I wanted to live my life. It seems so pointless without God. This wasn't an aha moment for me, just me waking up and feeling this incredible weight on my shoulders that I knew I didn't have to carry anymore. I was exhausted from living an empty life. I knew God would go with me into that pain and carry me out. I was rebuking the lie that God didn't want to carry those burdens for me, that he didn't care enough to heal my pain.

HER STORY ISN'T OVER

I am working on being a heroine, not a princess. Princesses have to wait around in towers, with pretty dresses and perfect hair. They are waiting for someone to come and rescue them. I am far more intrigued with the frontline of the battle than with the sideline pompoms. I am willing and *insisting* on engagement. I believe in keeping my voice and using it for his glory.

I love the picture above. It reminds me of how this girl became immediately more heroine than princess, as she took off her shoe to kick the ball even harder.

I struggled daily with wondering if he was ashamed of me and I was mad at him for that.

"But slowly I moved past the 'smite you' stage . . . and rested for a while at the point where I wondered if Max would ever reap what he sowed. Would he ever pay a price?

"Ultimately I realized that's not my concern. I will not move much further if I am fixated on him. Today I am on a new journey, not weighted down (most days) with bitterness. It's a journey of letting go, and calling on someone to pray for me, of blocking the lies by saying the truth out loud. Speaking the truth is like wielding a giant sword. It can cut down the lies remarkably fast, but you have to be able to hold onto it. And that takes belief and strength. It takes practice and will.

"And it feels like hope.

"Forgiveness is a choice I have to make every day. To realize Jesus died on the cross to forgive both our sins, and so, I can give it to God and just trust him to take care of it. It's become more about looking at Jesus and less about looking at what Max did to me.

"I now see I don't have to be defined by what happened. I am the sum of so much more than that. But it's still something I have to keep reminding myself. Even when I don't always know it, speaking the truth brings the eventual belief. That's what it looks like to take every thought captive. I haven't crossed any finish lines, but I can look back and see where I am today and that progress builds a quiet faith in me that there is a God who is moving me along this road of healing.

"One of the best parts of my healing is getting my voice back. I felt like I didn't have a voice during this whole season. When I look ahead to my future, I see a healthy Jill, surrounded by people who love her, and she is helping others. I had told the Lord recently that I was willing to share the very story I kept secret for so long, if it would help someone. And here he is, giving me this opportunity, and that breathes more freedom into me.

"I see hope, where for years I could only see a blankness. I am living more real now, more raw, and more authentic. Before, I always said, 'I'm fine. I'm fine.' It's funny how in some ways I will be a healthier version of myself as a result of this horrendous experience. It's one facet of how God will use what the enemy intended for evil and bring something good out of it. I am more sensitive and more truthful. I am more about relationship and less about rules. I would have rather learned those lessons in a million other ways, but accepting what happened to me is a part of this journey."

———————

I hugged Jill when we finished, sensing in her bravery and steely strength. It came at a high price, but I know God will use it. I wish I could see the rest of her life the way he can. I imagine it will be full of young girls trapped in situations they think no one would understand. I imagine her stepping into those stories and being a part of the redemption and the freedom that awaits them.

Relentless hope is not afraid of the dark; it doesn't want to push hard stories like these under the rug. God will use Jill as a lighthouse, sending out a beam of light he restored in her, to draw others safely away from harm. And I look forward to hearing those stories, stories of the enemy being defeated by the one he thought he had knocked out for good.

I have seen Jill feel swallowed by memories, guilt, shame, pain—the tricks the enemy uses to metaphorically grab her hair and push her under the water again and again and again. I don't know why I would assume he would be scrupulous, allowing her to catch her breath between dunks. He is anything but that. He wants to drown her.

Then there is this little pinhole of light she can see from her sinking position under the water's surface and it calls to her. It's hope. It's saying don't stay down there, push up, kick your feet; you want to breathe, fight for air, move, move! *MOVE!* Jill feels her legs moving and she fights her way to the light. A moment in that light, and the hope fills her with fight. It's time to reclaim and restore what the enemy was snuffing out.

Look up, look out; believe it's yours for the taking. It's not what has happened, but what you are capable of. It's relentless; it's hope. It's yours.

Take it.

4

*We were delighted to share with you not only
the gospel of God but our lives as well.*

I met Kenny on a dreary day during a Nigerian rainy season. He was a young orphan boy born with an obvious birth defect—he was missing more than one half of his right leg. It would make walking difficult if not impossible for him, although the caregivers in his orphanage had created some makeshift crutches, a walker to encourage his mobility. He was an active child, moving around with a scoot that seemed as if he might not even be aware yet of his disability. He didn't sit still and cry for a rescue; if he wasn't getting any attention, he would move to where he could get it. His movements looked efficient, even graceful, his arms doing the lion's share of the work.

When you first look at Kenny though, it's not his legs that draw your attention, it's his Julia Roberts smile. It seems freakishly wide, revealing big, white teeth, and draws you in, forcing you to mirror back to him the same gesture. I wasn't even sure what happy secret we were sharing the first time it happened, but I found myself grinning at him with abandon and then watched as one by one he made eye contact and used his Jedi trick on the rest of our team.

KENNY AND MARY

There was no one he seemed to have won over more than Mary.

Mary was a young orphan girl about Kenny's age and was born with no visible physical struggles. She was found as a baby outside of the gate, wrapped in blankets. As Kenny scooted his way around the concrete floor, collecting dust and whatever else had fallen down in his path, she wasn't ever far behind.

She modeled his every move, including dragging her perfectly healthy leg behind her.

When I talk to our missions teams about the children we serve, I often quote Beth Moore's illustration (originally told by Gilda Radner) of the pregnant dog that was hit by a car and lost her hind legs. She learned to get around by using her front two legs and dragging her behind on the ground. When her puppies were born, they came out with four fully functioning legs, but all of them in their first few weeks chose instead to walk like their mother and drag their rears behind them.

When I share that story, I remind our guests the children we serve are often simply modeling their only example. That's not an excuse for any problems they might have, such as poor performance in school, or aggressive behavior, or a tendency to lie, but instead it's a motivator for us to engage in their lives. We need to be another example and show them what it's like to run on the four proverbial legs God has given them.

Watching Mary drag her healthy extremity on the ground brought that illustration flooding back to my mind. I might not be crawling around on the ground, but I am undoubtedly crippled when I blindly follow anyone's powerful example. I sat down on a corner bench and watched them scoot around the room. I felt introspective and eventually convicted. *About what, Lord?*

My sister-in-law Corrie joined me on the bench and we watched them in silence for a while until I broke the quiet. "I'm feeling sorry for Mary, when the truth is, I think we are all a little like her sometimes. I know I am. I can unthinkingly read someone's opinion and adopt it as truth, not evaluating it or filtering it through my worldview. How often have I been

> The children we serve are often simply modeling their only example.

enamored with a person and compromised my conversation or actions as a result? When have I excused my impatience or lack of self-control because "that's just who I am"? Have I ever swallowed a political stance or modeled a judgmental attitude because everyone around me has? Am I or do I think for myself?"

I leaned back against the wall. *Geez, I thought today was about them. Lord, where is this coming from?*

Corrie listened and encouraged.

I watched Kenny and Mary and slowly moved onto the floor with them—straightening out her leg, putting some weight on her knee, hearing her protest, repeating my action. It lasted for a moment and then she dragged it again. I leaned over to where she was headed and straightened out her knee again. The metaphor claimed more mental mileage. *You, Lord, are straightening out my leg. Don't let me forget this moment.*

I was lost in my thoughts, welcoming the conviction.

I asked the Lord for insight. *Bring to my mind specifics—where am I dragging?*

I have a friend who recently challenged me on some of my theology. I was aghast, offended even. I have always thought like this; everyone around me thinks like this! I read books to remind me I am right about my faith, I sing songs that echo my beliefs, I am sure we are right—so sure, I am basing my whole life on this.

His criticism was that I talked like a Calvinist but lived like an Arminian. He said my theology was the spiritual equivalent of having my cake and eating it, too. "You say 'All the days ordained for me were written in your book before one of them came to be,'" he said (I often quote Psalm 139:16), "and yet provide passionate discourse on how every one of us has the free will to choose our salvation, so do it today."

Defensive, I began on automatic pilot to articulate the rhetoric I knew would make me sound intelligent. The only problem was, somewhere in the middle, I thought about Kenny and Mary. *Hmmm . . . did I come to this on my own? Did I hear someone else say it? Did I think this through, and if I didn't, am I crippling myself? I know there is a Truth Lord, and I know you are it. Will you walk with me and straighten out my leg if it needs it? Can you teach me to be more aware of my shortcomings and less opinionated about others'?*

It's been months since I have seen Mary and Kenny, and I recently learned that Mary is walking without assistance and Kenny is growing to rely on his walker. It's funny, how that report fills me with joy. I wonder when Mary first stood on her own two feet without Kenny's example? I wonder if she is playing a part in his willingness to be upright, which is inevitably slower and harder for him?

As a track runner in school, we used to run what were then called "Indian trots"—running in unison as a team, all in a line. Every quarter mile, the leader would fall to the back of the line, and the next person would move forward, setting the pace, cheering on those behind her, feeling for a moment the freedom of being the frontrunner.

Maybe Mary and Kenny were just running their version of the Indian trot, and now it was Mary's turn in front.

Wouldn't it be beautiful if, in our faith communities, we could learn to rely on each other in those ways? If the leader didn't always also have the tiresome jobs of pacesetter and cheerleader? If every once in a while, he or she had the freedom to fall to the back of the line (especially during a season of struggle, doubt, or loss) and let someone else take the lead? Would we see less burnout and crashes and more margin and longevity? And would we have less lame followers and grow more experienced leaders? Less opinion adopters and more original thinkers?

I have been thinking about the commonalities in the people I have identified as having a relentless hope. First, they seem beautiful to me. Serene, dignified, confident—they are unhurried, dynamic, flexible, observant, grateful. In today's headlines when Hollywood's beautiful young girls find themselves in heaps of trouble, we see them and can appreciate their exterior beauty. But not many of us are drawn to them. There is, in fact, something about their instability that repels. In contrast, the people whose stories I share in the following pages talk about their struggle, their God, and their resulting lessons in a way that, for a moment, can almost make me envy their plights.

NAOMI

I sat in a hospital room today with a girl I have known for more than a decade. This afternoon she gave birth to a son, though at eighteen, she herself still seems like a child to me.

Naomi has come and gone in my life, then come back again, on her terms and according to her needs. Her boyfriend died a few months into her pregnancy, and she has little support from other people. So she wandered in my front door months ago, looking for work, conversation, money, and sympathy.

Some of these I have in spades, some I have only a little.

Although she frustrates me by her lifestyle choices, the bottom line is I care for her. I first met her mother, who gave birth to Naomi at age sixteen, a number of years back. She was a mess then, and still is. Her poor choices have left her with scars, but the bulk of the price has been paid by her daughter, who is aimless, amoral, and penniless.

> Wouldn't it be beautiful if, in our faith communities, we could learn to rely on each other?

We revived our friendship over the last few months and I was struck again by this truth I am discovering. Our stories cannot be unwoven from our families very easily, and certainly not without a great deal of attention. Naomi admires her mother, whom she sees in a new way now that they share the teen pregnancy experience. She also resents her mother in the same old way, when she doesn't provide the support she so desperately needs now.

We talked for hours about making our own way, about not playing the victim, about pulling ourselves up and out, but I wondered, is her sheer willpower enough? Can anyone really reinvent their life out of pure desire? Does my friend even comprehend that she is living the exact same life her mother did—the life Naomi loathed her for?

Some cultures around the world value age, history, and experience. They focus on entertainment, relationships, and values that reflect an understanding of their past. Our Western culture tends to value youth and future planning, expansion and growth, development and new ideas. As a product of that culture, I can get excited about change and planning and what's still ahead. It's just in me. In an effort to be independent, (and bigger, more successful, more innovative, richer) we gamble with and can ultimately lose the understanding gained from others who have gone before us—especially when we discard their lessons as irrelevant.

We are also told (on talk shows, in therapy, in books) that we have the right to discard what is difficult. We don't have to be in a relationship that requires too much effort. But sometimes life without this effort, without this relationship, is actually harder than the work it takes to communicate, to understand, and to relate.

> Could I be enjoying the precious that was extracted a generation ago?

TWO LAMECHS

While reading Genesis 4 the other day, I was struck by the story of Cain, the son of Adam, who in his anger killed his brother Abel: Cain had a son named Enoch, who had a son named Irad, who had a son named Mehujael, who had a son named Methushael, who became the father of a boy named Lamech.

Lamech, in Genesis 4:23, said with his own words, "I have killed a man for wounding me, a young man for injuring me."

It seems safe to assume that controlling anger was never addressed in this family line, but one angry man trained up another

HIS STORY ISN'T OVER

T HIS orphan African baby is one of the 148 million orphans in the world today. Without intervention, he will be like the low fruit hanging off the tree; the enemy will recruit him before he's even old enough to understand there is a side to pick. Up to 90 percent of orphans end up in the black market and/or involved in prostitution. God is sending his Bride out for them, and giving us, as his hands and feet, dozens of biblical promises to fulfill: to not leave them or forget them, to execute true justice on their behalf, to maintain their causes, to lift them up, to be their Father, to hear them, to come to them, to make them a home . . .

and another, leaving behind a trail of consequences and at least a couple of recorded murders.

Contrast that story with that of Noah. Noah was the great-grandson of another Enoch, as recorded in Genesis 5:21-24: "Enoch walked faithfully with God; then he was no more, because God took him away" (v. 24). It was strength of character and unwavering faith that was passed down through Enoch

- to his son Methuselah,
- to his son Lamech (a different Lamech),
- who raised the boy who became the man who built the ark and saved the world.

Do we even know the names of our great-grandparents? I could only name two out of the eight. Among these genealogy-loving Jews, we can bet Lamech knew Cain's name and Noah knew Enoch's. Their stories and the manner in which they were shared greatly influenced and then grounded f these men.

started me thinking, what stories and family lore have been around my reunions and dinner table, and how have they shaped me? Could I be enjoying the precious that was extracted a generation ago? Was someone's strong faith before me born out of a hardship I didn't know about?

I kissed my friend's baby good-bye and left the hospital room. As I looked one last time into his newborn eyes, I said a quick prayer that his story doesn't pick up where his mother's and grandmother's have left off. I hope for something different for his relationships, his life. I hope for a season, a disruption, even a teaching somewhere down the line that causes him to pick up the pieces these strong women have handed him and appreciate their efforts, but not repeat or resent their pattern. And I hope for a shedding of the wounds that trap them all.

I walked down the dark hall of the cheap clinic and pushed open the door to the bright Mexican sunshine. As I raised my sunglasses to my eyes, I looked up and hoped my hope is enough.

ANTONIO

The first time I met Antonio was the night he and his siblings were dropped off at a children's home. I didn't even know at that point his painful story wasn't just beginning, it was already well underway. I wish I had that in mind more often when I interact with someone who is sad or hurt or angry—the idea that there have been lots of chapters already endured that have shaped the attitude I feel resistant to, or the edge I am put off by. If I considered more what has already happened in the day of the person I am talking to, and focused less on my perceived (mis)treatment, wouldn't I be more in line with a heavenly perspective?

Antonio's story started when his mother was erroneously accused of abusing a special needs baby she was caring for, even though it was she who took him to the emergency room, suspecting his young mother of inflicting the bruises. The baby's mother, Rosa, was a sixteen-year-old girl without a family. Antonio's family had essentially adopted her, so much so that Antonio referred to her as *hermana* (sister).

When the doctor confirmed the bruises were not natural, but the result of someone's infliction, they took into custody both Rosa and Antonio's mother. During interrogation, Rosa sold them a story of abuse, claiming Antonio's mother was mistreating both the baby and the other children. Antonio's mother, being held in a separate cell, only spoke one word when asked, "Who could have inflicted these bruises on the baby?"

"Rosa," she sadly whispered.

Antonio's mother lost that battle and consequently, was thrown into jail. The judicial system in Mexico starts from a premise that you are guilty until proven innocent, and so after months of futile attempts to clear her, and knowing it was one person's word against another, Antonio's father came forward and admitted to a crime he didn't commit. His heart and intention were that his wife would be released and freed to care for her children who were missing her.

But the police didn't believe the confession and, unsure of the details and suspicious of fraud, jailed both parents in response. It was at this point the children were moved into a government children's home, where they experienced separation, depression, and abuse.

Antonio's story would take him through several children's homes before he landed one Saturday afternoon at the orphanage where I was working. At this point he was nine and very angry. As all the children sat in the office, waiting to be processed, Antonio's older brother looked over at him and noticed a particular, familiar look on his face. He whispered fiercely, "Don't do anything stupid. Don't leave. We must all five stay together."

Antonio would say later he knew his brother was right even then, but it didn't stop him from fifteen minutes later making a break and running out the gates and down the highway, screaming and throwing rocks at the car that had just left them. Several people took off after Antonio, but out of everyone, it was his brother who was fast enough to catch up with him and repeat his sentiment. At twelve, he was the oldest of the five siblings and had honed his survival skills enough to know they had a stronger chance of getting through this most recent storm if they were together.

They had a stronger chance of getting through this most recent storm if they were together.

Antonio's years in this new children's home were marked by his hardened heart and angry demeanor. He bristled when given attention and was suspicious even of the slightest kindness. When it was time for him to graduate junior high school, the last year of required schooling by the government, he was faced with some choices: Would he turn to a life in the streets, trusting himself—the only person who hadn't let him down? Or would he accept our invitation to move in with one of our ministry staff families and enter high school, and potentially even college?

After a month of struggling over his decision, Antonio decided to come to our campus and live among us, but no one could say he lived *with* us. He was rebellious and repelled people on purpose. He would never initiate conversation and would only answer questions with the shortest answers possible. His house parents continued to have a soft heart for him and loved him with consistency and prayer during this long season.

It went on like this for years.

We often quote the apostle Paul when describing this style of ministry, "We were delighted to share with you not only the gospel of God but our lives as well." The gospel, lived out like this, becomes less a presentation and more a path to share.

> It is a Spirit thing, a supernatural switch. Not something you can program, or train, or twelve-step, or muster up.

As Antonio graduated from high school, we cheered him on to the university, where he began coursework in criminology. He studied martial arts and worked on campus, but mainly kept to himself.

Then this past winter, something made Antonio curious enough to agree to attend a youth retreat where, incredibly, he prayed to receive Jesus as his Savior. In that weekend everything about him changed, including his countenance and especially his attitude. It doesn't always happen that way; many of us have a slower, less remarkable transition between our old life and a Spirit-led life. But for some, immediate transformation can occur and be seen by all.

Antonio's life was immediately different.

Eight months later, I heard him share his testimony at a gathering of hundreds of orphans. He stood and said, with voice shaking, "If you lie in your bed at night and think no one cares, you are wrong. If someone tells you that you are not worth it, that's a lie. You are a child of the King, and so with that comes all the rights of his son and daughter. You are royalty and have a Father. Don't ever forget that. Allow that singular truth to set you free."

I saw Antonio out the other night, well past his curfew, hanging outside one of our teen homes. But there wasn't anyone in sight.

"What's going on?" I asked slowly, heart sinking as I wondered what I had caught him doing.

He looked sheepish. "I know I am out late. I'm just walking around the house, praying for the boys who live inside. I have been kind of hard on them until recently." He looked up, pleadingly, "I am just asking God to break their hearts, like he has broken mine."

Stunned, I muttered something about not making too much noise and walked away.

I thought about my friend Naomi and longed for this kind of transformation to happen in her.

Because this is how the chain is broken. It is a Spirit thing, a supernatural switch. Not something you can program, or train, or twelve-step, or muster up. It's God-directed and literally stunning to watch, and is not for any man to take credit for. This is how a life and a family and a generation is redirected and redeemed.

God is looking at who Antonio *is*, (and not what he does or has done) all in one sweep. He sees the baby, the abandoned child, the rebellious teen, the forgiven young adult. He sees him as the dad, the provider, the husband, the grandfather. But he is also looking at Antonio's son and grandson, who will be extracting precious character from the worthless start to Antonio's life without even knowing it. They will stand on the strength, the humility, and the grace Antonio understands uniquely from his story and that will become part of the family lore, a family mark. They will benefit from the hard work he is doing now and will experience many faith-filled, righteous moments as a result.

Antonio is not defined by his missed shots, by any means. He is the son of a King, a man who is just now learning all he was made capable of.

Relentless hope.

As I walked away from that exchange with Antonio, it was late in the night, and I looked up at the stars and found myself wondering. Is my perspective big enough? Do I even have the ability to get or gather all God is doing to restore what is broken? Can I see it? Am I asking the right questions?

I can get so tripped up on questions like "Where were you, God, while Antonio was being abused?" But I am trying instead to ask different questions. How will you reach down and make anything good from a world spinning out of control and filled with people hell-bent on destroying themselves and each other? How *do* you pull that good down through the generations so that it benefits someone not even present for the pain? How can you do all that and make sense and resolve anger and bring forgiveness? How can you see each of us and all the days we have experienced and the temptations we have succumbed to, and choose to offer us grace and mercy? How can I gain that set of eyes when I see someone? Lord, is that what it means to be seated in the heavenly realm?

I like the second set of questions better, they are less bitter, less like a pout. They sound more awestruck and hopeful. I am more expectant of a God I am curious about than whiny about a God I am shrinking with each complaint. I have spent a lifetime seeing pain with a one-dimensional perspective. The perspective that it's-all-about-me. The mistreatment by someone is about me (when maybe it's about them). The broken or failed job, relationship, or test creates inconveniences or embarrassments for me.

Could maybe all of it, the hard and the good, be what it is, and I can/am supposed to choose instead to seat myself in the heavenlies and wonder if he is interested in healing more than just the situation at hand?

Having my cake and eating it too? I don't know about that . . . but I am willing to change my questions, challenge my assumptions, wonder aloud to the Lord more than presume I have it all right. I will refuse to drag a leg just because I see others do it or because it is easier than standing on my own two feet and asking hard questions. Of all there is to grasp about the Lord, what percentage of that understanding have I accumulated? And how in the world can I question God when thirty years of studying and worshipping later, I am still standing on only a fraction of the knowledge of his greatness?

Lord, do what you will, and teach me to recognize it. I will lean in with my relentless hope that you have it all worked out in a realm I don't yet see. I will stand confidently on that small piece of understanding you have granted me and believe there is always more to the story.

That's not foolishness, that's not blind devotion, that's not even a cop-out to not have to think about it. It's a commitment to relentless hope.

HER STORY ISN'T OVER

J AZMIN, one of the thousands of students helped by Back2Back Ministries, is currently studying criminology. She wants to focus on criminal prevention. In her words, "Many times we can think we are doomed to repeat the family patterns we have witnessed. I am an example of how we can change them . . . my dad couldn't finish junior high school for economic reasons, but I have taken advantage of an opportunity given me (by God) to study. . . . I am a witness to the fact our problems and obstacles are not an end to our story, but the opposite, a beginning to a new future."

For me.
For Antonio.
For Naomi.
For Kenny and Mary.
For my challenger.
For us all.

Do I bring to the...
and not giv...

I pulled into a field, unsure .... I was
worshipping on this Sunday with a ... wn congregation, the
Evangelical Church of West Africa. Upon entering the rough-cut,
one-room sanctuary building, I was delightfully assaulted with the
sounds and sights and smells of Africa.

You never know when you sit down in church what piece of the
service God will use to stir you. Sometimes it's a beautiful moment
in worship, sometimes it's a stirring point in the message, other
times it's the quiet reflection in prayer, or a meaningful communion
table. This day, it was the offering. And I am pretty sure for me, that
was a first.

It started out as a beautiful song about a widow and her now required hard work to keep the family together. (In many third-world
countries, women know losing your husband often means losing
your children, if you can't find the means to support them on your
own.) The lyrics lamented in a minor key about the role she must
play as both mother and father, and the little relief she will now
experience here on earth. The group was singing in a combination
of English and Hausa, but there was enough of my language for me
to be able to enjoy both the rhythm and the lyrics.

Then a woman moved down the aisle and, as if performing a

skit, danced around the altar, using a broom to sweep the imaginary floor. Eventually she switched to a field tool as she "harvested," all the while never standing straight up, always bent over, emphasizing her backbreaking responsibilities. While she worked, we sang a chorus about this hardworking widow, who relies on her new audience of One.

Next the notes moved out of minor keys and there came a shift in the melody as the rhythm beat faster, almost to a chant. People sang louder as the words now addressed the church, those of us who were watching the widow. We were suddenly a part of the scene—the skit essentially widening, with all of us now playing the part of the village, watching her work. I could feel compassion rising as the noise became deafening. I wanted to reach out to her, to help her with the broom, to straighten her back, to pray with her, encourage her. *What must that feel like, that constant fear she won't have enough for her children now?*

As if on a cue they all knew (even though I didn't), the aisles filled with the women of the church, carrying on their heads bags

THERE is a website I watch (www.worldometers.info) which marks in real time various statistics of the world: numbers on society and energy, food consumption and disease. It's easy to look at the woman in this image in terms of numbers (she is one of the 1,030,752,464 undernourished people in the world today), but when you look at the picture and see something as small as the detail of her dimple, she becomes more than a statistic—she becomes someone with a story. What precious has she extracted? What has life taught her? What are her interests? What are her questions? What is her pleasure?

of corn, rice, beans, or handfuls of naira, the Nigerian currency, and they laid them down at the feet of this widow. It was akin to a special offering a church might make for a natural disaster or a visiting missionary, something above and beyond; although it was unlike anything I had ever seen. Technically, it was an offering, but it was way more than that—a combination of celebration, responsibility, and privilege all wrapped up in one.

Deuteronomy 24:19-22 records God's commands to the Israelites regarding the harvest:

> When you are harvesting in your field and you overlook a sheaf, do not go back to get it. Leave it for the foreigner, the fatherless and the widow, so that the Lord your God may bless you in all the work of your hands. When you beat the olives from your trees, do not go over the branches a second time. Leave what remains for the foreigner, the fatherless and the widow. When you harvest the grapes in your vineyard, do not go over the vines again. Leave what remains for the foreigner, the fatherless and the widow. Remember that you were slaves in Egypt. That is why I command you to do this.

This congregation was obeying the verses from Deuteronomy, but it felt less like a duty and more like a pep rally.

My mind couldn't help but flash to the offering box fixed to the wall outside of the sanctuary in churches I have attended and admired. So many of our churches today don't even include an offering as a part of the worship service anymore, lest we offend someone. We have taken pride in the fact we aren't asking for money in the American church, so that people can come and not suspect an ulterior motive, but are we missing out on this beautiful dance, this joyful release of our firstfruits in obedience?

The fulfillment each woman was experiencing as she handed over a part of her own hard work was contagious, it was worship. What a contrast to the scene in millions of churches that morning across the globe. Churches like ones I have sat in and more than once been guilty of reaching in my wallet and releasing what I thought was the bare minimum I had to give to keep my holiness intact.

I so wanted to join in the dance; I wanted to help that widow. I wanted to loosen my grip on what I had earned on behalf of those he has asked us to care for. I sat for a moment in my pew, sweating in the African heat, moving with a rhythm you don't hear as much as feel, and debating my next move. Grabbing some naira from my backpack and feeling both sheepish and compelled, I sashayed my way down the aisle, closed my eyes, and released what can never satisfy, to worship.

> "I'm so thirsty and the land looks dry, Oh, but I smell rain."

CRAIG

Last night at Teen Challenge, where singer/songwriter Craig Aven serves as a staff counselor, two men had an altercation that resulted in a trip to the emergency room. Tensions can run high on occasion, as men and women in this residential facility seek healing from chemical dependency. A bit sleep-deprived this morning, we sat down to talk about his life, and his own previous chemical dependency, but he started out sharing this incident with me.

"I just am afraid it will be a tailspin toward despair for these guys," he lamented. "I can remember so clearly what it felt like the morning after I made some stupid decision, the struggle to hear God, and the reoccurring feeling that the road back up was too long for me to climb again. I wrote a song last night about the period these guys are in right now—that in-between time when you start metaphorically building the ark (out in public), but there isn't any rain yet. You think to yourself, *I sure hope I heard God correctly.*

> *I'm so hungry I can't stand it,*
> *I'm so desperate as I wait,*
> *I'm so thirsty and the land looks dry,*
> *Oh, but I smell rain.*
>
> *I hear scoffers all around me,*
> *They tell me that my longing is in vain;*
> *They've given up and now they think that I should too,*
> *Oh, but I smell rain.*

Craig settled down to start his story, and emphasized how it began. "I was raised in a Christian family and honestly can't remember a season when I didn't have a heart for the things of God. Jesus was very real to me from an early age." When he made childish, poor decisions, he remembered feeling deep remorse. Recalling an incident with his mom, "I stood outside her door while she slept one night and just cried about how, earlier, I had rudely spoken to her. I hoped with my childlike faith that both she and God could see into my heart and know that I didn't really mean what I had said."

"As an adult man looking back, I realize it would be easy to blame my eventual chemical dependency on poor friend choices, or the easy access I had to it in high school, but I know, as I have walked through this recovery process, that I made some agreements in those early years. There were lies I believed about myself and about others, lies about God—all of them I carried around like burdens. Drugs became a way for me to feel happy and confident. I didn't have to worry about what anybody thought of me when I was high. They offered a sense of rest and security.

"The first time I really remember compromising, of sensing the Holy Spirit grieving inside of me, was as a child. I experimented with smoking at the bus stop. It gave me a thrill and I loved it. Even then, I could feel my appetite, craving for more.

"As a high school student, I had surgery to remove my appendix and tasted for the first time the relief a pain medication could bring. The first day, I took one pill as prescribed. The second day, I tried three together. That appetite was raging; I had tasted how good sin can feel. The agreements were solidly in place and the result was a perfect storm. I knew I shouldn't do it, but at the time, it was out of obedience that I thought I shouldn't—simply because the Lord had made a rule against it. Instead of wondering what he was protecting me from, or wondering where real relief was found, I began to resent him for the rule.

"I abused the refills, yet kept my addiction at bay through high school. I was living in part for the Lord: already leading worship in corporate settings, going on mission trips, and writing songs. The early tenderness I had for God was growing, but so was this dark side. I felt God speaking to me in this season, but I dulled my heart against the conviction. I tuned him out. And even after confessing

> "Those days it felt like a war inside of me, like I was constantly conflicted."

my sin on occasion and promising not to do it again, I knew (as did he) I still would.

"Secretly I had always wondered what kind of high I could get from cocaine, but I was too afraid to try it. The heart will harden though over time, and mine was moving so fast down that road, I couldn't even explain it. My addictions escalated and soon, cocaine had its stronghold.

"Those days it felt like a war inside of me, like I was constantly conflicted. The Spirit-controlled side hated the addict lifestyle, but in fear of losing my fix, I just used harder to quiet the conviction. I guess that's why they call it running. And run I did, so hard that I

HIS STORY ISN'T OVER

CRAIG'S story is multifaceted, but the image that sticks with me is of his mother, praying on her knees for a situation she understood was bigger than she could solve alone. I don't have a verse for this, but experience has taught me that there is no prayer warrior like a mother, and I have watched (on more than one occasion) chains be literally snapped during a mother's intercession.

started believing I may have crossed the point of no return. That's a favorite lie of the deceiver, and he was whispering in my ear over and over that my life was ruined and there was no way out or back. Eventually I believed that message, and if the Lord was saying something different in those days, I couldn't have heard it over that pounding noise.

"However, God in his mercy and with his eternal perspective on my life was looking into my heart and reading not just my sin, but also my intention. He was the only one who could see the heart I still carried for him, even though there was only minimal outward indication.

"I wanted out, and I told him, many nights as I went to bed wondering if I would even wake up from the overdose of whatever substance I was on. So the night I was pulled over for speeding and weaving between the lines, inwardly I breathed a sigh of relief. As soon as I saw the lights, I knew the Lord had sent them. He couldn't apply his light to that which I was keeping in the dark. I had six different substances in my bloodstream. The arresting officer asked me what I did for a living, to which I sheepishly answered, 'I am a worship leader down the road at a church.'

"He looked at me and tilting his head, asked, 'Is this any kind of behavior for a worship leader?'

"High, and feeling disrespectful, I responded with a smart-aleck comment, then sobered a bit to say, 'I don't lead worship because I am worthy, sir; I do it because he deserves praise.'

"At this point, my issue became public. I was forced to tell the pastor of my church and eventually its congregants, 'I have been consuming forty-plus pills a day for the past couple of years.' Inch by inch, I started to tell the truth. Part of what happens when you live in the dark is you become especially skilled in deception. The rebuilding process involved me having to tell the truth and accept help. I tried and wanted to live in light. I went to a hospital inpatient rehabilitation center. I had two men in my life offering intense accountability. I stopped working in ministry, found a different job, and soon after, much to my heartbreak, I started using again.

"*What was God thinking of me now?* I wondered. What could he have been thinking of me the day I sold my keyboard, which was the one object I had, apart from the pills, that brought me intense pleasure? I sold it for $750 and then blew it on drugs in the following days. I could only imagine what he was thinking of me, as I knew what I thought of myself.

"It was a season of constant worry that I was ruining my relationship with the Lord—forever.

"The truth is, looking back, I still hadn't dealt with the root. I just kept cutting off the branch at the ground level and it kept growing back twice as strong. I needed to ask myself, 'Why do I want to use?' But I didn't know what I needed. We build habits over the course of years, and I desperately wanted to change my circumstances and those habits. But God didn't want to change only my circumstances; he wanted to change my life, my understanding of him, and my belief about myself. He wanted me to see him for who he is and he wanted me to see myself as he did. And there wasn't a program or person who could do that for me.

"What was God thinking of me now?"

"The addiction wasn't fun anymore—a thousand times now I wanted to quit. But I was a slave to this sin. Literally, I felt in bondage.

"If you say yes enough times, you become the person who can't say no.

"In one of my final episodes, I walked into my parents' house high on cocaine and stopped short at the sight of my mother in her room, on her knees in prayer for me.

"I stumbled into my room and sat down on the bed, realizing more than anything, I just missed Jesus. That Jesus she was talking to, the Jesus I had sung for and written about, and who I knew in my heart had saved me. I had been ignoring his conviction for so long that I was out of fellowship with him. I know now that it says in 1 John that if we claim to have fellowship with him yet walk in the darkness, we lie and do not live by the truth. But if we walk in the light, as he is in the light, we have fellowship with one another, and the blood of Jesus, his Son, purifies us from all sin. I prayed and told the Jesus I had known my whole life that I did love him and I missed his stirrings, his comfort, and ultimately, his conviction.

"While I was praying that, the words *Teen Challenge* popped into my mind. I wasn't even sure what it was, but I knew the Holy Spirit had put it there. I opened my eyes, looked up, and answered out loud, 'Yes, I'll go.'

"'A Designated Wilderness Area' hangs over the entrance to Teen Challenge Cincinnati, with 'Deut. 8' inscribed beside it. I remember looking that up and feeling overwhelmed. The Scripture teaches that God brought his people to the wilderness to test them and see what was in their hearts, to see whether or not they would obey his commands. It was clear God was doing the same for me.

> "He broke me in a million pieces so that I could experience communion with him."

"Honestly, obedience had become such a burden because of my growing list of failures—when I read that, I felt crushed. I was so afraid when it was all said and done, I would only prove to be a failure. Looking back now at the same Scripture, I see it a bit differently. I don't think the omniscient God needed to test me so that he could see what was in my heart, but rather that I could see the truth about myself.

"Over the course of my nine-month journey through Teen Challenge, he exposed my heart—to me. He made me aware of the deep strongholds of disbelief and fear that were causing me to distrust his character. He broke me in a million pieces so that I could experience communion with him and get to know him as the God who is my Father. Hebrews 12:10 (*NLT*) reads, 'Our earthly fathers disciplined us for a few years, doing the best they knew how. But God's discipline is always good for us, so that we might share in his holiness.' This is the promise I cling to when I begin to doubt God's heart. As he continues to father me, I see more of his heart and have been learning there is nothing I can't trust him in.

"Now, several years after I said, 'Yes, I'll go,' I am full of hope. My heart doesn't want the counterfeit joy that drugs promise. It nearly stole my life, but I experienced enough of the sin to know it isn't satisfying. Today, he is the object of my desire. He is the lover of my soul. Only he can satisfy me in the deepest way. Everything else is shadows. The desire is not wrong. I felt bad for wanting to fill that desire. The lie I believed was that something other than Christ could fill it. God designed me and purposed me for a relationship with him. In his mercy, he wouldn't let me settle for anything less.

"I have stayed victorious by living in the light, but that doesn't mean the temptations aren't some days still real. On the days I struggle with remembering who I once was, or with believing lies I have long evicted from my heart, I see it for what it is, the attempt of the enemy to win again. To get more leverage out of old baggage."

I hugged Craig, like I have a thousand times before, as a dear friend. We have experienced much together as we have been working out our faith with fear and trembling. I asked him what he would want someone to know who was struggling to hear God's voice, who was struggling with wondering if God even was listening anymore.

He told me one more story: about a month into his program (after much repentance, honesty and brokenness), he remembered how it felt to be at peace after a season of turmoil. He was walking by himself from the prayer garden to his dorm on a cool, spring evening, and in an aha moment, he exclaimed aloud to no one in particular, "I am in fellowship with God. I can feel it!" For so long he had ignored the voice of the Holy Spirit and his heart had grown almost lifeless, but on this day, he could feel his heart inside of his chest, full.

He recounted how he couldn't believe he had traded such sweet fellowship for cheap counterfeits, such peace for a momentary high. "I guess I would want a reader to know that there can be peace after darkness, there can be a sensitivity again to the Spirit, there can be light—maybe that will encourage them?"

He smiled at me questioningly and I laughed, agreeing. "Yes, that will encourage us. Your story encourages me to believe. To trust in a God who takes the long view. Who is patient, and perfect in his timing, and who leads us toward events and miracles that remain yet unseen. It makes me worship at the feet of a God who looks at our brokenness and sees our intention. Looking at your life, Craig, your testimony teaches me that even when the land is still dry, I can learn to smell the coming rain."

Some of our pain comes from our own hands, like in Craig's story, where he walked himself into his own destruction—or did he? From a seat of self-righteousness, it would sure seem so, and it's easier to assume that. We think that about the homeless people we pass (which makes it easier not to stop); we think that about the young gang members (which causes us not to grieve each death); we think that about the prostitute (so when she loses her kids, we actually cheer).

But what if we could see them from Christ's perspective? I am sure we would see what factors made, for example, my friend Craig ripe for that type of trap and the spiritual warfare playing into the situation. But here, we don't have all that, so in order to reflect the heart of God developing in each of us as believers, we need to develop that muscle of empathy, so we don't give in to judgment (a tool of the enemy to destroy community and weaken our testimony).

I smell the coming rain for the widow in the African heat, which God is calling a church to see. I smell the coming rain for the addiction crisis we face in today's culture. I see God not looking at the

> What if we could see them from Christ's perspective?

situation from a long distance away, but seeing each person closeup. He is deeply personal. He models that for us in Scripture, so even if we don't feel it, we can know it as truth.

REHOBOAM

I love the kings from the Old Testament. Studying them allows us to see someone's life before it even begins, watch the factors at play as it unfolds, and then read with curiosity the consequences of their actions. I am fascinated by many of them, but one in particular captures my attention—Rehoboam. He was the son of Solomon, who was the son of King David and his wife Bathsheba.

Solomon had been ruling over the twelve tribes of Israel, then because of his personal missteps, was stripped of eleven of those tribes and left with just one—the tribe of Judah, who became the responsibility of Rehoboam when Solomon died. (All eleven of the other tribes of Israel fell to King Jeroboam.) Second Chronicles 11 records how for the first three years, Judah walked in the way of David and Solomon. Verse 17 tells us that initially Rehoboam strengthened the kingdom of Judah. Then in verse 18: "Rehoboam married Mahalath. . . . Then he married Maakah daughter of Absalom, who bore him Abijah, Attai, Ziza and Shelomith. Rehoboam loved Maakah daughter of Absalom more than any of his other wives and concubines." (Remember who Absalom was? He was the son of David who used his power to try to overthrow the king. Rehoboam and Maakah were first cousins.)

What happened to Rehoboam between years three and five? Women. (Same trap that got his father Solomon in trouble.) It was a land of his own destruction he walked into, but I imagine from God's perspective he saw uniquely how it was a weakness for Rehoboam. The enemy is watching our histories as well, and is waging a spiritual war around us tailored specifically to those hurt spots. Rehoboam married many foreign women who gave unwise counsel. He allowed the idolatry of their gods to flourish. Second Chronicles 12:1 sums up his story, "After Rehoboam's position as king was established and he had become strong, he and all Israel with him abandoned the law of the LORD."

> God doesn't discriminate between pain caused by ourselves or others.

During the fifth year of his reign, the king of Egypt came up against Jerusalem, which under Rehoboam's watch had forsaken the Lord with molten images and male prostitutes. As King Shishak of Egypt was coming for him (with some twelve hundred chariots, sixty thousand horsemen, and innumerable troops), the Lord sent his prophet to warn Rehoboam: "You have abandoned me; therefore, I now abandon you to Shishak" (v. 5).

Having been around prophets his whole life and seen the

wondrous things the Lord had done, Rehoboam recognized truth when he saw it, and he and his leaders immediately humbled themselves. God saw their reaction and responded, "Since they have humbled themselves, I will not destroy them but will soon give them deliverance. My wrath will not be poured out on Jerusalem through Shishak. They will, however, become subject to him, so that they may learn the difference between serving me and serving the kings of other lands" (vv. 7, 8).

It was soon after that the treasures of the temple were confiscated, yet Rehoboam and his people were not totally destroyed. The people understood firsthand how blessing follows obedience. When they served the King who had their best interest, he took care of them; when they served other kings, they lost provision.

How true that lesson is for me today!

I wonder if in the aftermath of those chariots and horsemen and troops, as they were sitting around without the full tables of food they had experienced under David and Solomon, and without the beautiful treasures, if it was tempting to call their state cursed, or blame their enemies. The truth was, they were sitting in a field they had sown themselves.

Hosea recorded the words of the Lord (8:7): "They sow the wind and reap the whirlwind." Rehoboam wasn't the victim of a curse; he was a victim of his own sin. And as a leader he took many others down with him.

But what I am in awe of is the fact that God doesn't discriminate between pain caused by ourselves or others. He doesn't choose to redeem or extract precious from only those who find themselves in difficulties of another's making. He sees both my friends Jill and Craig as his children and wants to heal them, love them, forgive them, grow them both the same.

Waiting for the rain to fall in Africa.

Following in Christ's footsteps means I must do likewise. I am to love the one who is hurt with the same capacity as the one who did the hurting. If I am a reflection of the Father's heart, I have to be up for giving grace, a listening ear, and a seat at my table to all.

I recently was in a conversation with a youth pastor of one of our country's largest churches. He was sharing with me his journey, which included a recent divorce and a season of pain brought on by his own choices. Immediately following that period, he lost his ministry job and put his resume on a Christian job board. Then he got the call from this large church.

"I was so surprised when they called. I thought it was a joke. After everything that had unfolded in the last couple of years, I thought I would be lucky to get a volunteer position in ministry, let alone an interview at a church as prestigious as this one."

"Were you honest?" I asked him, "Did you tell them what had happened?"

"It was all in my cover letter; they already knew when they called me. At the final interview, I asked the senior pastor what in particular led him to me. I knew he had a whole stack of other, more qualified choices. The pastor looked at me and said, 'Son, we have found in the church that most people have a season of brokenness, one way or another. We like to look for staff on the other side of that broken season; we find it makes them better ministers of the gospel of grace.'"

I left him, wondering if that pastor's thinking is the key to their high attendance more than any creative programming or fancy speakers. He sure sounds like the kind of person I'd want to spend my Sundays with.

I'm wondering in reflection how I can put this all together—can I live with the release of my firstfruits in worship, not reluctance? What does it look like to sashay down the aisles of my day, letting go of more than what I want, to receive more than I could ever need? Can I live like I'm smelling rain in a drought? Would I/do I build arks in my life? Can I live with perspective, missing the traps the enemy sets specifically with my name on them? And then when I get caught in a trap, or see someone else there, can I be a girl of grace, not judgment? Can I live as a minister of this gospel, inherently seeing the same value in a broken man as is reflected in his shiny counterpart? Can I live with that hope?

My response almost feels like a tiptoed, leaning-forward, "What's next?" kind of posture . . .

All I do know is, I am all in.

COMING AFTER ME

Whether you turn to the right or to the left, your ears will hear
a voice behind you, saying, "This is the way; walk in it."

—ISAIAH 30:21

The water was unbelievably green and deep blue. "This is so beautiful," I said aloud to myself. I looked down and my legs were another shade of blue, bruised all up and down. I could hardly feel them because the water I was standing in was so cold, they were numb. We had been swimming and hiking, jumping and falling all day. I looked over at Marlen, our foster daughter, who was watching—waiting for the moment she could let me know exactly what was on her mind.

"I'm not going any farther—I mean it, Beth, not another meter!" Marlen said. "This is crazy! This isn't a hike, it's—it's like . . . a survival course." Her voice was getting louder. "And I am not going to survive!"

"Whose idea was this anyway?" I joked with her, tousling her hair and trying to coax a smile. "Did I talk you into this, or did you talk me into it?"

We had been planning for weeks to hike Matacanas, an all-day canyoneering adventure that traces a river up a mountain and involves dozens of jumps into water, miles of hiking, and a climb up a waterfall. I thought it might be fun to bring some of our teen girls and had visions of team building and bonding.

I admit it. I had been secretly delighting in how hard it was for the girls. It was, in some weird way, fun to watch them get pushed to their limits and then hold their hands when it was hard. My friend Julie and I had been cheering them on all day, talking about fears and our own limits. I kept saying, "When we have nothing left, we are still full of the riches of God. He alone can carry us through." It was a sermon in motion, a lesson played out all day as we pushed our bodies to perform and our minds to conquer fears long held.

"When we approach a cave, just swim through it. You might feel something brush your leg, but it is just a plant. In the darkness, don't let your minds play tricks on you." Ryan and Juan, our guides, were wondering at this point what they had agreed to. Our group was comprised of two women and six female students, not their easiest bunch, I am sure.

> When we have nothing left, we are still full of the riches of God.

We talked each other through the cave and sat on a rock on the other side for a minute, discussing the darkness.

"I don't like not seeing what might be coming for me."

"I think my imagination is worse than reality, I would rather know what's out there."

"I felt calmer when she took my hand."

"I liked praying in the darkness, knowing God is light."

We went around the group and talked about how it felt to be afraid. "Faith will carry you through any fear," I told them. "Take a hold of someone's hand, yes, but know that God himself is standing there beside you."

Marlen and I went on to talk about faith, and how various Bible characters might have been afraid facing a giant, or in a lion's den,

COMING AFTER ME 97

and what role their faith played in staying calm. Did it swell before they picked up the rock, after it was slung, or before it hit? What about as the giant fell? When the lions were nearby, but not hurting him? When he got out and was safe?

When we trust in God, can we count on a faith rush in time for the test? as a reward for the test?

I could hear the water roaring up ahead and was focusing on our conversation as we came upon the waterfall.

"We will be climbing up this waterfall freestyle," Juan instructed. "Each of you, one at a time, will be attached to a rope; so if you fall, we will catch you and just drag you up." We were all a bit intimidated as we peered up the thirty-plus-foot wall of water. One at a time, the girls began to ascend and eventually scrambled over the top and out of my view.

Marlen and I were the last ones left at the bottom. I had been treading water for a while and was not interested in giving a long pep talk. She had also been treading water for a while, and was not interested in climbing. We were at a crossroads.

"Marlen, please go. You can't stay here. This is the path out. The longer you wait, the weaker you will be."

She just looked at me—unsatisfied, tired.

Finally she grabbed the rope, locked eyes with me, and said, "The faith rush doesn't come first." Then she made her way up the falls.

At last, it was my turn. I started up the rope. The water was coming down so fast, my arms were feeling weaker and weaker. I made it halfway when I lost sense of where I could put my hands next. I stopped, but the water didn't, and as it crashed against my face, I started to have trouble breathing. I looked up, but couldn't see anyone over the edge of the falls. I imagined them relaxing up there, waiting to see me climb over the top. Only I couldn't move.

Am I stuck? afraid? I thought to myself. Juan said if time passed and we didn't surface, they would just pull us up. I was sure they would start pulling me up any minute. But I waited and didn't feel any tension on the rope. *They aren't coming.*

I thought about Marlen and her comment about faith before we need it. She was right; we don't get an extra measure in advance, we get it just in time. *Oh, God! I believe in you; I have faith you will come for me.* I felt my breathing start to change. I was relaxing in the midst of my fear. But the water didn't stop and now I really couldn't move. I was calm, but I was still stuck.

"Beth, are you OK?" Juan shouted over the roar of the water.

I turned and looked up at him. "Where did you come from?" I asked slowly. *Are my words slurring?*

He was hanging on the rock and reaching out for me. "When you didn't reach the top, I decided to come in after you." He had free-jumped down the falls and then climbed to where I was, all without a rope. He then proceeded to guide me to the top, where I found dry ground and my breath again. After a round of hugs, a Power Bar, and ridiculous promises to Juan of homemade cookies and unlimited babysitting of his daughter, I had my wits again.

> I learned that he will always come after you.

"Marlen, you are on to something. If God swelled our faith in preparation, there would be no need for a test. When God fuels our faith in the midst of a trial, it becomes a growth step. He longs for us to cry out to him, to ask him to show up. The rest of day, when we are about to jump, or climb, or push ourselves against a fear, let's rush into it—almost leaning into it, knowing he is always on time with his strength. Holding back until faith musters itself up is just a waste."

At the end of the day, we sat on rocks, nursing our wounds and retelling the stories of our adventure.

"I learned risks are easier done in a group," said one girl.

"I learned I don't like heights," laughed another.

"I learned you can keep going," said another, more seriously.

"I learned that he will always come after you," I added quietly.

GREG

Isaiah 30 doesn't start off so well. "Woe to the obstinate children" is the message from the Lord. The next seventeen verses go on to relate how the children of the Lord had refused to follow his instruction and had gone their own way.

But in verse 18, we hear this: "Yet the LORD longs to be gracious to you; therefore he will rise up to show you compassion." God goes on to tell his people that he would answer their cries for help, that no matter where they turned—*right or left*—he would be there. His voice would always be there, telling them which way to go.

HIS STORY ISN'T OVER

THERE are 1.3 billion people today without clean drinking water. "For I was hungry and you gave me something to eat, I was thirsty and you gave me something to drink, I was a stranger and you invited me in" (Matthew 25:35). Countless organizations around the world are working to remedy this situation. How could you partner with one of them and bring hope to a child like this one?

We get so used to waking up and knowing which way is our office, our classroom, our favorite coffee shop; we go our own way, simply because it's what we do. I can forget to listen for his voice until I am deep into my day. Or until I am in trouble. I miss out on so much story that way. I miss plot twists and suspense. I miss adventure and risk. By the time I remember to ask what he wanted from me on any given day, I might have missed out on the best version possible of that one day. And I'll never get it back.

But still I am comforted by this one truth: There is no place I can venture, either in obstinacy or obedience, that his voice can't still be heard, telling me which way to go.

"This is going to be a difficult conversation."

I have been studying a bit about wilderness lately. I find it fascinating the Jews saw it as place of strengthening and today I see it as a place where I am weakened. I want to believe more in what God can do to me in this wilderness and believe what he says in Hosea, "He allured me there to speak tenderly to me." I met recently a man who has spent some time in the desert. His wilderness came in the form of a job loss, and he lost that routine of knowing where to step each day. But his story (with the plot twists and the suspense) and his questions that followed—Left, Lord, or right?—grew and stretched his faith and, in listening to him, mine as well.

"About a year and a half before I lost my job, our company was bought by a group of investors. When that happens, everyone always wonders, *What are they going to change?* I was a part of a team that assured the employees everything was going to be fine; this was an opportunity for more growth. By the end of the first year, we had done a whole series of things to grow the company, including creating a new position which I eventually held. Now I was functioning as the COO, and with this new role came new responsibilities, a new salary, and a whole host of new pressures. I remember feeling hesitant, knowing this would draw me away from customers, but ultimately, I felt it would be a good experience for me professionally.

"As a leadership team and as partners, we built a company we hoped to double in size. We had no way of knowing that in the near future, without much warning, the economy would blow up. We thought we were ready, but in truth, we weren't. About every forty-five days, we were making job cuts. I personally laid off well over a dozen employees. Sometime in June, I proposed to my colleagues that I return to my old job. I was a significant cost on the company, my position made sense if we were doubling in size, but not if we were stepping backwards.

"I knew the position was in jeopardy, but I never suspected that *I* was. I was a partner in the company. I had worked there for a decade. I sincerely never expected to be told I had two weeks' notice. The conversation began with my boss, and I immediately recognized an opening line I had used myself, 'This is going to be a difficult conversation.' Fifteen days later I was gone.

"My first reaction was: 'I don't think we should end our relationship here. What if we . . .' I was brainstorming, negotiating, trying to see what I could do to salvage the situation. I sent out an e-mail to a handful of trusted Christian brothers, asking for a conference call. I wanted their insight, encouragement, and wisdom. I put it all out there, so they would have the information they needed to give sound advice. I was sharing my plan and pleas when one guy inter-rupted to say, 'No, Greg, I think it's time. Let it go.'

"My heart sank. I knew he was right.

"I sent a note out to about a hundred guy friends:

> *On Monday, Jessica, Zak, Karen, and I returned from our annual mission trip in which the central theme was SHELTER. We were able to see firsthand how God meets the daily needs of some of the most impoverished folks on the planet.*
>
> *So it's with new faith and now, some new humility, that I inform you that my professional position will be eliminated on July 31. We learned this news to-day, and the rest of my company will know next week. Karen and I would appreciate your prayers for a positive and swift conclu-sion to the job search, as well as increased unity in our marriage during this difficult period for us both. I'd appreciate your ideas and assistance.*
>
> *I really am excited about what God has for us next. He is good and trustworthy. Anyone can be faithful in good times; now's my turn at bat.*
>
> *Peace,*
> *Greg*

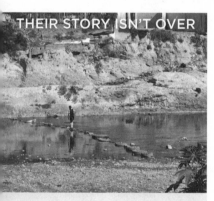

THEIR STORY ISN'T OVER

Across the world, unemploy-ment is rampant. The tempta-tion is to remedy unemployment with generosity. And although generosity is a virtue (and a com-mand), could we possibly be send-ing a message to those we love that work is bad? Could we in-stead garner resources, empower each other, network, and toil be-side and collaborate together to the end of less relief work and the beginning of more development?

"The stated purpose of my note was to gain prayer and networking, but primarily just prayer. I knew enough to know I needed plenty of that. *Where do I start?*

"Two weeks later on July 31, I had my last day of work, and at 5:30, I walked away from an office and a vocation that had dominated my last decade. At 6:00 my good friend Paul dropped off a bottle of wine, and we shared a small toast celebrating what would be the beginning of my inevitable new work.

"It was a simple but hopeful gesture.

"From the beginning, I always had a lot of hope; I am the guy who wakes up with the cup half full. One door closing was another opening. But telling my wife was especially hard; she was shocked. She did a really good job keeping her chin up, but she wakes up as a realist. I had to apologize for putting us in that situation."

"We hadn't gone without a paycheck in seventeen years."

There was a long pause, as he fought for composure. "I am sure she wanted to remind me in that moment that she had asked me to reconsider my new position well before this latest development. She had concerns with the toll the adjustment to the new COO responsibilities would have on our family.

"She would tell me much later, although shocked and heartbroken, a part of her was relieved.

"And in the way God does, he used this incident to clean up or clear out some hidden minefields in our marriage. One of the toughest parts about this stage was forming our budget. We didn't agree on financial priorities before I lost my job, but my high income hid that defect in our marriage. Now we needed to negotiate this issue under the worst of circumstances. But the result? More connection, more intimacy. Wasn't that what I had put in the letter to my friends as something I wanted?

"There were plenty of tests of that connection. One of the hardest was the day of the last paycheck in October, with no job in sight. That was a tough week. We hadn't gone without a paycheck in seventeen years.

> "I begged God for clarity and comfort; had I made the right decision?"

"Although nothing came up immediately, and it was easy to lose heart some days, what helped was seeing God go to bat for my family during this time. I was let go on a Tuesday and the night before, my fifteen-year-old daughter and I discussed the possibility of her attending a private Christian high school in our town. I liked the idea she was interested in a healthier pool of friends, and with my salary on that Monday, it shouldn't have been a problem.

"But the next day when the game changed, I had a choice to make: do I still send her and follow up on the leading I sensed the day before? Or do I react to my new circumstance and become more conservative in my spending?

"After praying as a family, we decided to still send her. Even unemployed, we didn't qualify for any partial scholarships. Humbled yet again, I spoke to the finance director in the school, and between the arrangements I made with their office and someone coming through and offering a donation toward her tuition, we were able to still make it happen. I wanted, needed evidence God was still there for me, and this event was a tremendous encouragement.

"There were so many opportunities during this process for the enemy to wreak havoc with my thoughts and embed his lies in my vulnerable heart. He was saying, 'You are lazy; you aren't doing enough. Maybe there's not a job for you out there.' I would wrestle to hold on to God's truths and remain hopeful. On those especially difficult days, I would find someone calling to encourage me, or ask me questions about the process—prompting me with accountability questions and a fresh perspective. I often hung up the phone or left a meeting feeling like those connections were timely, like God knew what I needed and when.

"Karen was tremendously supportive. There were only a couple of times when she became frustrated and impatient with my search approach: I was spending too much time on Internet networking sites and not enough time meeting with people. Whenever Karen and I had issues, I would struggle to start my day. It was in those couple of desperate days that I just begged God to do something—like find me a job or fix an issue with our marriage. These were the times I thought that I could dig ditches, as long as Karen and I were together and right. It was a tremendous reminder to me of what I really cared about.

"The turning point came around the start of the new year, and I was now heading into my sixth month unemployed. I had been to meetings, interviews, and networking coffees. I had copied resumes and endured well-meaning advice. I finally received an offer, a good one, but not the one I was hoping for.

"I heard in my head the counsel of a friend after I had shared with him that I wasn't going to settle. He reminded me my family needed to eat. I was in the interview stages with another company for a position I was far more enthusiastic about, but I hadn't heard anything definitive. I got to the point of needing to make a decision on the first offer and I was asking God for his wisdom. *Which road do you have for us, Lord?*

"Ultimately, without any security, I felt led to turn down the job I could do, but never wanted. I begged God for clarity and comfort; had I made the right decision? I went another two weeks without knowing. My cup-half-full perspective was being challenged. Finally, mercifully, I received a call. The man talked on and on about a variety of details surrounding the position and the company, and I waited, barely breathing until I heard the words, 'We are making you an offer. You can start middle of January.'

"In the end, I was unemployed five months, and I know for some it is better and others experience worse. I just know, waking up every day, I was forced to ask God to provide for my family and myself what I so effortlessly thought I could do on my own. I was asked over and over the same question. Whether always well-meaning or not, I don't know, but regardless of its intention what I heard was 'What are you going to do?' in every conceivable form.

"I started out answering with my job search game plan—details of networking sites and headhunter meetings. But then over time my answer changed. I started saying, 'We are praying—asking for peace, joy, direction, and new opportunities.'

"The truth is, now I am fully employed in a position I enjoy and I don't want to stop asking myself that question, and I don't want to stop answering with that game plan. I want to pray for peace, joy, direction, and new opportunities, no matter what my vocation is. I want to seek God's face and heart and plan for my family in the valley and on the mountaintop.

"I can see in hindsight that God pushed me out of the nest. I knew that I needed a change, but I kept ignoring the signals and hoping for the best. I didn't want to deal with the uncertainty, broken professional relationships, and effort associated with changing jobs. Looking back now, I know that I was holding myself hostage to a situation that was unhealthy. It was in his mercy he led me out.

"One of my favorite verses during this time was 'Lord, to whom shall we go?' (John 6:68). I identified uniquely with Peter's words to Jesus. In my own way, I was asking the same question, although mine sounded like 'This is my breaking point, God. I have nowhere else to go.' I would meditate on that verse and realize, what alternative do I have? I can't hide from the truth that Jesus is God and he's brought me to this point for a reason. Should I stop believing in God because of my circumstances? Can I stop believing in the truth? No, that would be as illogical as not believing in gravity.

I can't unring that bell. I know the truth: Jesus is God. For me, there is no way around it.

"I spent a few days feeling guilty about thinking this way. It's not a very loving way to think of God, as sort of 'You're my only choice.' But I love Jesus' response to Peter: 'Have I not chosen you, the Twelve?' (John 6:70).

"God was pleased Peter could see the truth, when so many others missed it. There's specialness about Jesus' relationship with his twelve disciples. He was so proud of his workmanship, and ultimately that's how he feels about me. I guess the truth is this: I would be happy going down in flames, just knowing that my Father is proud of me."

A change in perspective, a humility of heart, a demonstration of community, a release of pride—these are just some of the shifts I saw in Greg as he recounted his story. He never let go, that's what most encourages me. Whether he finally relaxed into God's love and plan for him, or actively pursued it, the result was the same.

Our days and steps and activities are not made up by our own whims and plans. There is a Storyweaver, who moves his principle characters into other chapters for multifaceted reasons, some of which we won't be privy to until Heaven. The people who Greg meets now, the impact he will have where he is today, are all part of a plan he could submit to kicking and screaming or accept with grace. Greg demonstrated for me a spirit of submission to a plan that wasn't all about his own comfort, but ultimately was for his own good. That's the plan of a God I can lean into.

So in response, I ask today, "Right or left, Lord?"

> *The Fear-of-GOD is a spring of living water so you*
> *won't go off drinking from poisoned wells.*
> —PROVERBS 14:27 (*THE MESSAGE*)

"Keep going, everyone. I am sure you are almost there!" I cheered half-heartedly. I was coaching a small group on a team-building ropes course and everyone (including me!) was frustrated. I was sure there was a point to our current challenge and believed our other staff member when he said it was possible to solve, but my patience had worn out along with my bug spray, and my cheering was waning in the afternoon sun.

The goal was to have two people, connected by their hands, balancing on two separate thin wires about a foot off the ground. The two wires form a V. The two people must stay on the wires from the bottom point of the V until the top, but as the space between them grows, so does the challenge. At the end of the V, the space between the two players is about nine feet wide.

Pair after pair attempted the challenge, but everyone failed.

"How's it going?" My friend, our guide, approached us. I looked at him woefully.

He leaned in to me and whispered, "Do you want to know the trick?"

I nodded. Of course I wanted to know the secret, if there was one! I was ready to be successful.

"When you start at the point of the V, focus all your effort on keeping your partner up. Don't think about your own balance or self-preservation. As you focus on his balance, and he simultaneously on yours, you find equilibrium." We spread the secret and sure enough, within minutes every pair who had previously failed succeeded without much struggle.

It made for interesting conversation on the way home: if we focused more on holding up our brothers and less on our own fears of falling (or who was looking at our perceived fall), we would inevitably reach our goal—any goal—with less effort. How many more people (family members? friends?) could we keep up on the wire across from us? And when they do step off, do we find a new partner and move on, disgusted with the failure? Or do we stop our own journey long enough to grab our partner's hand and help us both regain balance?

> "Don't think about your own balance or self-preservation."

Years after my first experience on the Grand V, I took a friend to see it. I knew the trick, and had seen many people be successful, but I hated that I had never made it to the end. It was my little secret, as I taught many others to walk down the wire. I confessed this to my friend and he seized the opportunity to help me grow.

We started on one end, and I found myself suddenly nervous, curious if we could make it. I wanted him to see the concept at work. We weren't very well matched, in height or strength. I giggled as we began, already making excuses for an anticipated failure. We fell, as I expected. My giggling stopped; I felt bad.

"Let's try again," he offered, not willing to give up.

I stood up at the beginning point and slid my feet slowly on the wire, realizing I had more balance than he did. This is helpful at the beginning. He had the strength, which we were going to need near the end. I felt bolstered as I realized my role.

Visiting group members in Mexico practice leaning in on the Grand V.

We slowly pushed our hands together, crossing the point where we had fallen before. I closed my eyes, wanting to focus and not fail. Such a small-scale failure it would have been, but the yearning for success was very real.

I opened them, realizing the challenge had just stepped up a notch and the wires felt like they were separating rapidly. My friend was leaning in toward me to the point that if we fell, he was going down hard. I was still in self-preservation mode, bent at the waist—definitely not leaning in, and still not sure what I had to offer.

But seeing his risk moved me. In response, I counterintuitively leaned in, and together we inched our way to the end.

"Yes!" I practically yelped when we crossed the finish line. "We did it!"

He smiled, satisfied—the way men are when they meet a challenge.

I smiled back, satisfied—the way women are when they sense a connection.

Who is across from me in the Grand V of life, and do I appreciate the risks they take on my behalf? Do I allow them to talk to me honestly about the struggles they see in me? Do I ask them often enough to pray? Am I leaning in, straining for their success? Does it matter to me as much as my own?

A STRUGGLE

"I can't get over it," I sat down with a friend to process what I had been learning as I met with people for this writing project. "Everyone says the same thing, in their own words and ways, but everyone whose difficult life circumstance comes as a result of their own hands thinks their problem is the deal breaker. That if everyone knew their sin, they would never be allowed to lead a study, share a testimony, lead worship, volunteer in children's ministry, go on a mission trip, whatever."

I slammed down my diet Coke emphatically, "It's so the enemy's tool—to divide us, to make us feel like we are the chief of all sinners, to want us to be disqualified. I can only imagine God is heartbroken when we focus on our failures and not on his redemption."

My friend was quiet; I thought she must be processing my comments. She bit her lower lip and looked at me questioningly.

I plunged ahead, "I mean, what is the gospel, if not for broken places? I love that God is our defender!" I am quite the outward processor and can begin preaching at the drop of a hat, so I was off and almost running when she interrupted me.

"Beth, it's not that simple. Can I tell you something? a story? *my* story? about the Defender?"

I said yes, and seeing she was already shaking slightly, I sat back, deciding no matter what, I meant it.

———

"As a child, I was always ornery. I really just wanted to make people laugh, since I knew I was funny; but sometimes, it came across as ornery. It first felt like a compliment and then eventually became part of my identity. I remember loving wrestling with my brothers and climbing trees. I was a tomboy, and I liked it that way. When the neighborhood kids (both boys and girls) would come over and play house, I would volunteer (I actually don't recall whether I volunteered or I was just told to play that role because I obviously wasn't super girly) to be the boy. The boy seemed more fun; he was the protector, and he got to play with his shirt off. I simply remember wanting to be a boy and not liking being a girl. I loved the sense of adventure. When I was young I didn't think girls could have great adventures like I dreamt of, because my view of a 'woman' was something I disconnected with at a very young age.

"I can remember wanting to please my mom and make her happy—trying to with gifts, writing her little notes. But I was always cautious with her. (I felt burdened as a child about her, hyperaware of her state of emotions and our family environment.) Not like my friends, who were all over their mothers and affectionate. I could tell, even at a young age, she wasn't very happy. So I mostly kept my distance, and in all my childhood pictures, she looks mad and depressed—maybe it was because my father was

THEIR STORY ISN'T OVER

I hesitated only slightly in deciding to include this young woman's story of struggle. I knew it would make some people uncomfortable, but that momentary discomfort seems to me to pale in comparison to the long-term pain our brothers and sisters with same-sex attraction endure. My prayer is that we would hold the posture of open hands, welcoming all to join us at the foot of the cross.

the one taking the photos and she could not stand him! Even in late elementary school, when I learned of my parents' forthcoming divorce, I thought, *If this divorce will make her happy, let's do it.*

"All that childhood drama left me craving attention, female attention specifically. I both avoided my mother (I saw her as weak, disrespected, miserable) and longed for her to notice me, to pay attention to and hold me. It didn't seem as clear to me then as it does now, but all that combined together made me ripe for sin and deception. Unknowingly, I walked right into a relational minefield.

"I was a junior in high school the first time another girl admitted her attraction to me. I was shocked (but maybe happy?). I didn't know what to do, or how I felt, so I treated her horribly, but then followed it up with flirtation.

"When physical contact started between us, I was shaking. I was scared. But I was also hooked.

"During this time I was involved in a high school youth group, and so I did what I knew was the right next thing to do: I told someone there in authority. She was the first person I felt like I could truly trust with my secret. She responded great. She was one of the first ways God 'spoke' to me during this season. He used her to tell me the truth—that I was going to be OK, but that I needed to back away from that relationship. I already knew she was right, but she just confirmed it.

"Wish now, I had listened.

"The problem was, I was good at hiding things. This woman was the only one who knew about this awakening struggle in me—not

> "Unknowingly, I walked right into a relational minefield."

even my closest friends suspected. Even after that first relationship came to an abrupt end, the struggle and the attractions were still there. I was fighting it. I always felt this was true of me in my soul and didn't know how to deal with it. I was so conflicted and just became very quiet about it, which made it all the more difficult to have real relationships—the very thing I was most longing for.

"I went on to choose a Christian college and when I first arrived, I felt free of my struggle only because I wasn't seeing anyone anymore. But the temptations were still there, just not as strong. I felt 'healed.' While maintaining close female friendships, I dated men; I loved getting attention from them, but it didn't last long.

"As time went on, though, I could feel the struggle of same-sex attraction returning, and I distanced myself from my friends, skipped my classes, and spiraled downward. I knew I needed help, so I told my secret to my RA. I think I hoped she would be like the first woman I told. Although she was both kind and caring, out of 'duty' she felt like she had to tell our school authority. But I suppose I knew in my heart that keeping it hidden wasn't working, so ultimately I wasn't upset. I just didn't feel comfortable with other people knowing my stuff. The university had me sit through some counseling, which bore little fruit—just made me determined to change on the surface.

"If I could chart this struggle, it had been slowly climbing (most of the time without my realizing it) from those early days of role-playing as the boy. Now it was leveling off, I had a boyfriend, and I felt a huge sense of relief.

"The truth is, during this season, I still thought my problem was my sexuality, when that was only a symptom. The real struggle was my ache for attention and affection and somehow my mother was tied into that. So while I was trying hard to wrestle inappropri-

MY STORY ISN'T OVER

"So speak encouraging words to one another. Build up hope so you'll all be together in this, no one left out, no one left behind" (1 Thessalonians 5:11, *The Message*). Every time I speak, right beforehand, I say two prayers: First, Lord, let me be truthful and not impressive. Second, let this gospel truth leave no one behind.

ate thoughts into submission, my heart's real longings were left unattended.

"Although I had crushes, I only had one major relationship as a growing believer that was deeply inappropriate. But its scars run deep. I can still feel them, and I understand today the power of felt consequences when living outside of God's design. I let my emotions be engaged where they had no business, and I allowed a physical attraction to morph into the emotional attachment I had been so desperately seeking. I was wanting in the short term to feel alive; so much so that I eventually tuned out the God who was living inside of me. I distanced myself from him. He spoke to me all the time and I plugged my ears. He even tried to get my attention in my dreams and I brushed them off. I hated myself and didn't care.

"During this season, one of my family members 'came out,' and he knew about this private struggle I had. He said things to me I wish I hadn't heard. Lies I longed to hear, and that took years to unravel from my soul. As I was walking through this confusing time, I wish I had been more careful who I listened to. I didn't have the filter to know the lies from the truth anymore; I was just looking for evidence to support what I thought I wanted.

"I wish, Beth, I had heard the truth in this time." She looked up at me, and I recognized how hard this had been for her to share—the stopping and starting of the memories, the occasional glances to see if I was shocked. The questioning look she has even now, wondering if I will be repulsed or compassionate.

"What do you wish you would have heard? What do you remind yourself of now? Is this . . . still a struggle?" I asked.

"Is it still a struggle?" she snorted. "Yes, it is a struggle, but I am experiencing freedom in it, real freedom from it most days. The days I remind myself that I don't have some mental disorder, that I am not ill or repulsive or danger- ous even, and that God under- stands more than I think. That he will not abandon me or condemn me. That he saw me as a young girl when these longings for iden- tity and attachment began, and he understands the journey I have been on.

> "He is relentless about healing my heart and these wounds."

"He has been walking it with me and continues to be my safe place to rest in. He cares far more about what he and I have been talking about on this journey of healing than he does about my specific past sins. He is relentless about healing my heart and these wounds. He is so faithful and ever present. I have begged him to take this away more nights than I can remember. But if he had just removed it, I would have missed the conversations with him and the revelations he has given me about the true intimacy I can expe- rience. He has a lot to say to me about far more than my sexuality. He sees my darkness, all my pain, all my turmoil, and he shows me refuge and complete safety in him. It's beautiful and far exceeds anything I've ever tasted in my life.

"See, I used to think God hated me, was maybe 'over me' in a sense. The deception and shame I was under was unreal, stronger than anything I have ever experienced. The same-sex attraction I was feeling was really a longing, a place only God can satisfy. We women want connection. I wanted connection, and women were the safest place I knew to find it.

"Now from this perspective, it seems so clear. Every time I tried to get out from under this sin on my own, I failed. The Holy Spirit is the only one strong enough to break that bond. There is freedom, but you have to really, really want it.

"I won't ever go back down that road. I was under deception. I was out of fellowship. Today, I am in the light, with fellowship, and in community. It's amazing how clearly I can hear God in account-ability. I am now tuned into the right channel, not shutting out the voice calling out to me, speaking over me with his songs of love. That sin door named same-sex attraction is shut, it's locked, and I will not open it. I refuse. Can I still want it? Yes. I can be curious, but I pray, cry, confess. Taking the thoughts captive—it takes lots of discipline. It's a lot of fighting; it can be exhausting and doesn't always seem fair. But I have a new and healthy fear of the Lord, and if I went that way again, if I scratched that itch to sin, there are many people who would be fighting for me, because today it's in the light."

I had finished more than my diet Coke by the end of her sto-ry—a box of tissues and my Bible with its promises were also on the table. I just looked at her, a found sheep already among us ninety-nine, yet often feeling on the outside. Is there a setting where she can safely share this? Are there enough of us who appreciate that the path she walked toward intimacy with the Lord is no different than the one we've walked on?

I hugged my friend and meant it. I am proud to stand with her on the Grand V challenges of life. I felt like in a real sense, we made it to the end of the challenge with her testimony—as she leaned in with vulnerability, I leaned in as well, without judgment. She felt that and pushed even harder, as I did the same. How many times has she wanted to share that part of her story, and feeling weakness on the part of the person on the other wire, or in herself, just stepped off instead?

The enemy has the same game plan, over and over. He wants to steal from us, kill us, and destroy us. He did some of all of that to this young woman and wants the scars she now bears to be all we see when we look at her. The trouble is, I have a new goal—to have eyes that see things from above. And all I see is a fellow sister.

Truly I tell you, if you have faith as small as a mustard seed,
you can say to this mountain, "Move from here to there,"
and it will move. Nothing will be impossible for you.

—MATTHEW 17:20

Todd and I have a large family. It was never the intention, and I couldn't even begin to trace back how it all happened, but here we are now—a mess of people who love and are committed to each other and who live together most days in a little yellow concrete house. Two of those people are our foster daughters, sisters we have loved and battled for, going on more than a decade. Our story with them has been chronicled in other places, but can be summed up with one word: *perseverance*.

Doesn't matter what it looks like from here; this story isn't over yet.

We have persevered through a failed adoption and settled into long-term foster care. We persevered through a rebellious adolescence and are gratefully on the other side with a more mature young lady. We believed in and hoped for the redemption of a lost girl who finally came emotionally and spiritually home about two years ago.

Today, these sweet girls are treasures to us, but it's from this testimony that I originally quoted to myself, to the girls, to Todd, to the Lord, and to anyone else listening: "Doesn't matter what it

Barbara Shaw, opening up her painting.

looks like from here; this story isn't over yet."

One hot Sunday last summer, we sat in the open-air church at the top of the hill in my Mexican neighborhood, singing "Te Doy Gloria." It was a loosely structured service, populated mostly with the children in the orphanage down the hill, unprogrammed as far as services go, but it could take me to a place of worship faster than many other places I have visited.

The service finished and people lingered at the back before heading to their chicken stands and taco bars for lunch.

"Beth, do you have a minute?" I turned around to see a visiting guest, Mark Shaw, waiting for my answer.

"Oh sure, of course." I glanced around, quickly sizing up the patience level/approximate meltdown time of the children around me. I thought they had a few good minutes left in them. "What's going on?"

He started to tell me a story about his mother, Barbara Shaw—a woman I had never met, but when he said her name, it rang a bell. I remembered people mentioning her before in the context of prayer. "Barbara Shaw is praying for our trip," or "I'll pass this along to Barbara to pray for."

All this was running through my mind when Mark interrupted my thoughts to say, "She passed away this last year."

Oh. "I'm sorry for your loss."

I wasn't sure what else to say.

"Someone a couple of years ago gifted her a painting from a collection at one of your fundraising banquets. Do you remember those?" He plunged ahead.

I remembered. Some young girl from the Midwest had contacted me, wanting to use her art skills for orphan care advocacy. I told her she could paint something and send it down to hang in the children's homes, she could come down and teach kids to paint, or she could paint some canvases and sell them, sending us the proceeds. She ended up doing a little of each, but asked me for a stack of photographs for the paintings she was going to sell. She chose some to copy onto canvas. Then we auctioned them off at our annual banquet that year.

Mark continued, "Someone bought one of those for my mom and it hung in her house, where she prayed for the two children in the painting on a regular basis. As she neared the end of her life, she told me that she wanted the painting to come into my home after she was gone, and she wanted me to continue praying for the children. Something in her said there was more work to do and she wasn't sure what that looked like on the 'other side,' so I gave my consent.

"Since she has passed, I have been praying regularly for the children, but I don't have my mom's gifts. I am not sure what to pray exactly, and I find myself saying the same thing over and over. So I was hoping . . ." He paused, a pleading look on his face. "I took a picture of the painting and I brought it with me for you to look at. Could you give me some background on the kids, just so I can pray more specifically?"

I panicked inside. *Lord, what if I don't recognize them? I mean, the girl's a good painter, but facial features? And it's been years, what*

if the children have moved on and I don't know them? I can tell it's
important to him, Lord, help me know them!

I nodded my agreement. "Show me the picture, and let me
get my children, because they will know more of the kids collec-
tively than I will. Let's see if between all of us, we can recognize
them."

I called them all over and they moved to my side as he pulled
out his picture. We all looked at it and stared, stunned.

I finally gasped and tears filled my eyes, which were full of recognition.

Our foster daughters turned into me, burying their heads in
each shoulder, and we all looked at each other and then back at
him. "It's them, Mark. It's these girls. We recognize the photo-
graph that it's been copied from."

He looked as wide-eyed as I did.

The sweat beaded on my forehead as I wound up to preach to
anyone within earshot, "Do you realize that your mama co-labored
with us in the salvation of these girls' souls? That the Great Shepherd loves them so much, that as he set out on the trail to seek the
one sheep here separated from the flock of ninety-nine, he enlisted
in the battle a prayer warrior from Ohio, who was actively engaged
in orphan care without ever having set foot in this country. Now
tell me, when exactly did she start praying?"

Comparing notes, I began to recount for him the last few years
of their lives, specifically how God had wooed the oldest to himself
a year and a half prior to that.

We looked at each other and I exclaimed, "Now back to your
original question, the answer is yes. I sure do have a long list of
things for you to pray about!"

MARTHA

A while back, years after our foster daughters had settled into our family routine, an extended family member of theirs, who didn't seem to have their best interests in mind, came around threatening to disrupt our family unit. She was against our faith, our nationality, and probably my hair color, shoe size—you name it. She was making a lot of noise that she was going to use their shared family heritage to have them removed and placed under her full-time care.

In some situations, this would have been an answer to prayer, but in this case, without going into detail, it was cause for great alarm. The girls were worried, I was concerned, and those feelings together rose to panic level when she called one afternoon. She told me in no uncertain terms that she was going to come the next Friday with the authorities and remove the girls from our home.

I knew that once we could sort things out with any authority, they would see the stability the girls had experienced in our care and would note the lack of involvement of any family of origin up until this point. Because of this, I wasn't worried about the long run; I was more worried

HER STORY ISN'T OVER

MARTHA is no stranger to opposition, both physical and spiritual. Orphan care advocacy is opposed, as is all work of the gospel. Luke 21:15 (*The Message*) promises, "I'll give you the words and wisdom that will reduce all your accusers to stammers and stutters." Martha tells me the remedy of opposition isn't puffing up to be stronger; it's humbling yourself enough to admit your weakness, so he can become your strength.

about the interim and how traumatic it would be for them to be taken away.

So I called in reinforcements.

"Mama Martha" is the near saint in her seventies who had raised the girls in her children's home until almost five years before this, when they had come to live with us. With her slow, articulate speech, her gray hair and impeccable manners, I thought she would be my ace in the hole. Should someone come making false claims, she could set anyone straight.

> "Don't you ever forget, this is the only sword you take into battle."

I called her and asked, "Will you bring all your files on the girls: visitor logs their family never signed into, kindergarten records you had to fill out, yearly reports—anything and everything to show that this latest 'interest' is not entirely sincere?"

"Of course, Beth," she answered, "I will bring what we need and be there beside you in case they follow up with their threats."

Martha came to my home as promised, shortly before we expected any trouble, and she patted her bag in response to my raised eyebrows. "I have everything we need." She smiled.

Sure enough, shortly after, a small entourage pulled up and started making a lot of noise, which we moved inside to our dining room. Everyone had a seat as I tried calmly to broker an agreement about the girls and visitation, but no one was feeling in the mood to compromise. The girls sat there, eyes wide open, watching the whole show. Things started to escalate, and I looked at Martha and opened the door for her to speak. Surely she would know what to say, right? "I think Martha has brought some things for us to consider," I started.

She smiled at me and then bent down to reach into her bag. I felt better immediately. We had ammunition.

She pulled out her Bible (not the files I had asked for) and opened it to Psalm 1. I looked at her and fought the urge to roll my eyes, but respected her. Everyone waited quietly—who was going to interrupt this senior with an open Bible? She read calmly through the words and I could feel myself relaxing. She finished the passage about a tree planted by streams of water and looked up; she had changed the rhythm of the room.

Now hit 'em, Martha! I silently pleaded.

She looked at me, as if reading my mind, and averted her eyes to the page, starting in again, "Salmos 2. Por que se amotian las gentes, y los pueblos piensan cosas vanas?" She read the rest of the chapter and without taking a breath, moved into Psalm 3, then 4, then 5, then 6 and 7, on to 8 and into 9 . . .

We are in a spiritual filibuster! I giggled to myself.

Psalm after Psalm she continued to read until she was through 10, which ends with

> O LORD, You have heard the desire of the humble;
> You will strengthen their heart, You will incline Your ear
> To vindicate the orphan and the oppressed,
> So that man who is of the earth will no longer cause terror.
> (vv. 17, 18, *NASB*)

Then she looked up at our guests, who by this time were shifting nervously in their seats. (What's that verse about the Word of God dividing even joints and marrow?)

Lowering her reading glasses, Martha peered over them at the ringleader, "These girls don't belong to me any more than they do to this American couple, any more than they do to you. They are daughters of the Most High King, who loves them and speaks to them directly. Why don't you ask *them* where they want to live?"

Our guests looked at the girls and with frustration demanded in a loud voice, "Where do you want to live?"

The girls spoke their first and only word of the meeting. "Here," said one, and "Here," followed the other.

The entourage stood up abruptly and moved to the door, speaking angry words in their departure at whoever was listening.

I turned to Martha, wanting to celebrate what felt like a victory. I reached for the girls, and looked over at her, but her look stopped me cold. Sensing she had my attention, she grabbed her Bible and waved it in my face, seeming now far more concerned about me than our departing guests.

"Mi hija, don't you ever forget, this is the only sword you take into battle."

This hija will never forget, no worries. Life lessons do that to you, they stick. This one reminds me that it isn't ever what I bring to a table that saves the day. It's not my mouth, or my contacts, or my money, or my position, or whatever other idol I can fill the blank in with—it's my God, and my pleas to him, and the Word he's given me and on any day, that's more than enough. God sent two women, from two countries, four decades older than me to remind me: the battle is always his.

This story isn't over yet.

Since my encounter with Martha and the waving Bible, I have been trying to use this theme when tempted with any despair. I have been listening for him as he whispers it into my ear throughout the day or the week. I hear him asking me, Are you praying to me about this, or just obsessing about it yourself? Are you wielding the sword I have given you, or resorting to weapons of a lesser grade?

Martha and Barbara had a power I want; it's a power that recognizes it comes from another source. It's a power that is fueled by hope. Barbara prayed, hoping (which is different than wishing) in a Lord who was acting in a way she couldn't see. Martha stood strong, hoping (which is different than daring) in a God who has never let her down. Relentless these women are, and relentless I want to be.

Relentless hope has a fierceness about it, but it shouldn't be mistaken for ruthlessness or inconsiderateness. The fierceness represents the seriousness with which we face our opposition in this world. It's a fierce way of praying, a fierce way we stare down the lion circling the prey, or a fierce entrance into a fiery furnace. A kind of standing-your-ground that refreshingly isn't dependent on the latest polls, the opinions of others, or even a track record. It is instead a fierce hope in the one who has already accomplished all that is needed to bring peace and grace into a chaotic world and a confidence we are on the right team.

THE HERODIAN

Jesus knew a little about opposition; he had an opponent in his day named Herod. Herod was decreed king of Judea by the Romans in 40 BC. He was most known for trying to kill the infant Jesus by ordering the slaughter of all male babies under two years old in

Bethlehem. He was, among other things, utterly brutal and bent on displaying his grandeur and power. One of the peculiar ways he showed that was by building his own mountain, the Herodian, where he had a palace and is believed today, by many scholars, to be buried. I have crawled around on that mountain in Jerusalem and have wondered how many bucketfuls of dirt it took to create. It felt very Tower of Babel-ish, just another man's attempt to prove he was on the top of the world. Herod must have felt very threatened when Jesus taught a crowd the following truth.

As Jesus stood within eyesight of the Herodian and spoke about how it takes the faith of a mustard seed to move the mountain, he was talking about far more than topography, he was talking about opposition. I imagine him pointing to the mountain as he spoke and waving a mustard seed plant in his hand. He was constantly in his ministry and life in the shadow of that mountain, but its presence did not define him or his ministry activity. He never played defense, he was always on offense. There is no one, no government, no person who can stand in the way of God's work; it simply cannot be thwarted.

> I can be stunned into inactivity by my own mountains of opposition.

I can be stunned into inactivity by my own mountains of opposition and tempted to spend energy moving them bucket by bucket. God tells me in the face of his power, mountains can be moved with his Word. From the beginning he has shown us this struggle's outcome has nothing to do with what we bring to the table—it's all about what he has already accomplished. Paul emphasized the point in his letter to the Corinthians when he penned that if we have faith that can move a mountain, but have not love, we are nothing (1 Corinthians 13:2).

The method of mountain moving is a blend of faith in the one who can do it and love for those watching (and being moved). No one wins if I have an encounter like the one with the group I mentioned above and then gloat about their departure; I need to be as broken by their lostness as I am by the suffering of those I love around me.

JAKE

I had Martha and Barbara and Herod all swirling around in my head on the day I met with the following friend. I was curious what it would look like to hear his testimony and not think about what he had lost, but to instead think on what he could hope for. Or hope in.

I invited him to get comfortable and then he laughed, saying it had nothing to do with which chair he chose in the room, there was nothing comfortable about baring your hurt places. I waited, wondering if I would have the courage to ask the probing questions or just sit back and listen. I knew a bit about his story, I knew he was a young man with a broken heart. I knew he was rebuilding. I knew it was still hard some days. I knew he was trusting again.

Sighing, he looked at me, earnest, almost willing me to believe this doesn't define him. I have seen that look over and over by now. It's a determination to fight back for a life he wants. I have grown to admire that determination, to try and practice it in my life in the smallest of ways. A bad phone call or interaction will not ruin my day. An ill-timed conflict will not ruin this dinner. A fender-bender, a bill, a lost game, a slow Internet connection, a whatever . . . it will not claim/dominate/ruin this moment. I will look up and move on. It's my way of exercising in the small ways this muscle I have seen in such big ways in those I have interviewed.

I could see he had fought back for a life he believes is his.

I smiled, looking forward to hearing how God showed up and off in his healing. He started his story. "I think my happiest moments with Sara were spent in a restaurant, going over our days. I suppose it was because I didn't have to convince anyone at that time, not her, nor myself, that the life we had was what we both wanted. We looked like a happily married couple in the restaurant booth and in that moment, we felt like that couple. We were alone in a crowded room of strangers and yet known to each other. It felt intimate, and that should have been a clue, since that isn't really intimacy at all.

"If I were honest, I had doubts from early on in the relationship. Why I suppressed those and didn't follow those questions out to their logical conclusion was the single largest source of my anguish when it was over. I had hoped it was enough to simply hope she would change. I believed erroneously my faith could be strong enough to create change in her, to make her into the woman I wanted to marry. I lost sight of how personal our faith journeys are and how independently we stand before Christ.

"I dated her for almost two years, and we fell in love. A heart loves who it wills; it doesn't think, it just feels. She wanted to get married, I loved her; we had attraction and even my private doubts couldn't stop that train. I look back now to how vulnerable I was. I didn't have anyone being honest with me during this season.

"Supposedly the other people in my life also had doubts, but didn't know how to share them without offending her or me. I am mad now that they didn't tell me how they felt; there was a lot more at stake than our offense.

"Our short marriage was plagued with conflict. I remember thinking *Is it always going to be this hard? Is it this hard for everybody?* I constantly struggled with whether I was a godly enough man or offering her true wisdom. Why didn't she listen? She wanted to live her own life, even in the midst of starting her new life with me. I wanted to be one, and would sit at home on the nights she insisted on being out with friends and wonder how marriage could be so lonely. I hoped and prayed someday I could turn things around—that I could be godly enough to change her. I had seen it happen firsthand and wanted that testimony for us.

"Even when I felt angry or alone, I honestly still wanted things to work out. We would be in the middle of the same exact argument over and over:

> Her: Why aren't you letting me live? Why can't I make my own decisions?
>
> Me: Why aren't you happy here, with me?

"I would sit down with her and ask in a civil tone, 'Can you do this for me? Can you not go drinking? Can you not stay over at a friend's house?' Why did I have to beg to keep her around? Why didn't she want to spend time with me? Isn't a wife supposed to sacrifice certain things if her husband thinks they are detrimental to the relationship?

"These questions ripped into old rejection wounds I had nursed for a while. I hated how her actions could put me in a bad mood. I would be angry and hurt and withdrawn when she returned. Stress when she was leaving; stress when she came back. Tension was evident in most of our conversations.

"Then she would cry and not want to face the consequences of hurting me or our relationship. She honestly couldn't understand

OUR STORY ISN'T OVER

CENTRAL PARK WE LOVE YOU
LOUISE AND WALTER

THIS last year Todd and I were in NYC, walking together through Central Park. We came upon the most beautiful little pond surrounded with benches, and filled with people who were coupled up. The bench we sat on had this plaque, "Central Park We Love You, Louise and Walter." I found it terribly romantic that Walter and Louise commemorated their love for each other and this special spot in such a public way. In our crazed culture that hardly allows for an occasional date night, let alone a special place to return to again and again with our loved one, I found refreshment on their bench. I realized why they must have come here frequently. I am on the lookout for a "bench" for us. I want to lean into my partner when the battle comes, not make him my battleground. I want to leisure beside him for hours so when it's time to work, we are well rested.

why I didn't give her the freedom she craved. I honestly couldn't understand why being away from me felt like freedom. But then I would cave, moved by her persistent tears, and we would reconcile. I'd give her an ultimatum, and she would say she wouldn't do it again—whatever it was—but always would.

"I am sure this sounds destructive, but it was our normal.

"Eventually, I saw I was trying to fit a square peg in a round hole.

"Eventually, she knew she never wanted to be around, or at least not with me.

"The day she moved out, I was relieved. It was two days after her confession of unfaithfulness, to the man who is now her husband. She would still come back and say she loved me. 'I love you, but I don't love you.' What does that even mean?

"I would always want to get to the point, 'Enough is enough—stop talking around the issue. I want answers.' But there wasn't anything she could say to fix what

I knew was broken. Today, I am a divorced young adult. It was my biggest fear, and now I am a statistic.

"It was on the day of the divorce I finally emotionally pulled away from her. The judge lit into us about her disgust at our short and failed marriage: 'I have been married for twenty-nine years,' she started. I saw my wife and realized all her recent manipulative gestures were not hopeful; they were to keep me on the back burner. That's not a marriage; that's not something that holds together for twenty-nine years. This pattern had no hope of changing. Frustrated because I didn't come here to get lectured, I looked over at the woman I married and said loudly, 'Forget it. All of it.'

"And we departed, marriage dissolved.

"I wanted to understand why I felt the way I did. I spent less time mad at her and more time disappointed in myself that I let it go this far. I allowed her/it/love/pressure to sway my judgment. In the end, we were only married for nine months.

"As the marriage was coming to an end, I talked to my father and brother a lot. I talked to my pastor; every week we would meet. He didn't sit me down 'bullet point' style; he just let me talk and process through things. He gave me wisdom and not demands. He would say to me, 'Jake, I think you should not talk to Sara for one whole week. After that, if you want to call her you can. I think you will see how much you have grown despite what your mind tells you.' He gave me emotional stability. 'You made the decision to marry her based on emotions,' he would say. 'Let's talk about your history of emotions.'

"That was no fun—walking through a childhood marked by a basic lack of self-confidence. I was made fun of a lot, for being overweight as well as for being a pastor's kid. I wanted to find someone who wanted to be with me, who would cover that fear up. The betrayal of her unfaithfulness only enhanced my sense of rejection. I felt like everyone saw me for who I was becoming: the twenty-four-year-old husband whose wife left with another man.

"I lived in that land of false identity for a while after she left. My mind was heavy, my conscious was heavy. There was a thick darkness around me. Everything I thought about would remind me I was cheated on, I was left—I wasn't loved the way I wanted to be loved.

"I would journal to God and I wasn't afraid to yell out. I wanted comfort from him and yet, at times, I didn't want to have anything to do with him. I definitely grew tired of hearing my Christian friends write off the cause of our divorce as being 'unequally yoked.' I just wanted to hear that it would all be OK (with or without her).

"One powerful moment in the immediate aftermath was an exchange with my older brother. I respect him, and it meant a lot when he first saw me after our separation. With tears in his eyes he said, 'The Lord loves you, he will get you through this—it's not your fault.' Then we hugged. It sounds like a cliché, but it meant something significant to me, because I knew he was sincere.

"I prayed all the time. I would get up and start my day with great expectations, reading Psalm 139 daily for the first month. I wasn't afraid to ask people to pray for me. I just wanted to be fixed. I wanted all the trauma and emotions to go away.

"But as the days went on and the loneliness deepened, in my struggle I turned to alcohol to numb the pain. I would drink a lot to fall asleep. Then I would wake up frustrated, knowing the alcohol wasn't making me into the person I wanted to be.

"One evening, for the first time, I went into work drunk. That night, tired of the cycle of destructive emotions/drinking/conviction I was in, I started bawling—it went on for an hour and a half. I almost didn't recognize myself. I was acting so out of the character God had worked in me.

"*Who am I?* I had never thought I would be capable of acting that way. Sitting there, crying, discouraged, I began to pray, *God, I can't do this anymore. I want it all off my chest; the pressure is excruciating. I don't want to worry about it anymore—not the cause, and not the consequence. I don't care any longer what she does. I just want it to be over.*

"It felt like God was speaking to me, releasing me. I felt weightless. I realized God was not observing me from afar, he was feeling my emotions alongside of me. Intimacy between us strengthened and the fog and darkness began to lift. A quiet lie that had been building in my heart was replaced with a hopeful truth: I still have something to offer.

"I just wanted to hear that it would all be OK."

"The next step in my healing was consciously telling the Lord I was willing to be single, and then meaning it. I knew I had some growing to do, and one area God singled out for testing was patience. I had a myriad of opportunities to verbally lash out, to physically fight, to have casual sex, but resisting all of these traps developed in me patience and strength. That restraint grew into a grace that led me to my new covenant relationship with the Lord.

"I am dating now again. It was hard. I had to be honest with God; I couldn't have my heart broken again, and so I begged him to protect me, give me better discernment this time. I knew I would have to explain all of this to the woman I was with and trust that, if she was godly, she would see it's not who I am anymore, but yet it's still how I got here. That alone would take someone committed to God, and was in part, my litmus test.

"I am a different kind of man in a relationship now. I am less controlling and more observant. I am less interested in plotting the steps of the woman I care about and more interested in what the Lord is leading her to do. I am realizing that's the freedom that comes within commitment, not freedom to blindly act without regard to your partner, but freedom for each to develop as God directs."

I commented to my friend that he sounded like he was in a great place, and I wondered how he managed reoccurring old memories that threatened his peace. He responded, "I think it's natural to think back on what has happened. But I realize now the 'what ifs' can't be answered to anyone's satisfaction. It just is what it is. When a memory tries to crowd in, I think about what I can be thankful for—for example, we hadn't started a family. I give myself permission to have a bad day every once in a while and then I place it before God, believing he will clear my conscience, and better yet, renew it to something that is ultimately glorifying to him.

"I can find myself in situations where I feel almost provoked and definitely tempted to give in to old, familiar, negative feelings. My best defense in those moments is to pray without ceasing. I had to change old patterns of thinking. I had to change out my bed. I had to change my view of women. I had to sacrifice and wrestle to take my thoughts captive. All of that ground I have gained, I don't want to throw away.

"The people in my life who don't want to talk about what's happened are curious to me. It almost seems that they are afraid it might happen to them, like they might recognize themselves in my story. For me, there's only one reason to share something so personal and private, and that's so others can see themselves and learn. It's not because it feels good; it's actually very painful. I share it because I wish someone would have shared with me. I want to be bolder now with those I love when I see warnings from my perspective that they can't see from theirs."

——————— ▬▬▬ ———————

I finished the conversation thinking *Thank God! We have Jesus.* He is the only one not trapped physically and emotionally in the despair of the day Jake went drunk to work. Jesus sees the chapters in childhood that led to a poor partner choice and a doomed marriage. He sees the rejection and the sweet offer alcohol made, lulling Jake to ignore conviction and accept compromise. He sees the young man who has a new strength, who will be a far better husband now than before. He sees the dad who will some day welcome someone into his family with a colored past without judgment. He sees it all—not stuck in any chapter, not judgmental of his actions, not wringing or throwing up his hands: "What are we going to do with Jake now? Ruined!"

He has perspective on all events and is a God we can lean into and find comfort in and take direction from. He is a God extracting precious intimacy and growth from this worthless pain and pointless marriage. He is a God whispering, shouting, encouraging, and singing over Jake, "Your story isn't over yet!"

There is relentlessness to that kind of hope, and I hear the common thread in Jake's voice that I have heard in others. It's a voice of someone who has seen the darkness and fiercely stood up to it. It will not win; it cannot overcome. It tries to stand in opposition of the good work God is doing in us, but its gains are temporary and its scars are just opportunities to share how God has healed us. I wish we shared those scars more often, I wish Jake had seen someone else's before he plunged into a relationship not built on the Lord.

I wish for us, standing in the shadow of our own Herodians, feeling the frequent heat of the opposition, that we would remember the lesson of the mustard seed, and the power we have in Jesus' name.

9

SEEING SOMEONE'S PAIN

Everything exposed by the light becomes visible—
and everything that is illuminated becomes a light.

—EPHESIANS 5:13

I want to be a truth-teller. I want to live authentically—saying what I mean and meaning what I say. It's a struggle for me sometimes; I can relationally take the path of least resistance, fearing a short-term consequence that pales in comparison to what happens when I bend my opinion or silence my voice or look the other way.

The following story has been for me an example of someone who endeavors in her healing to tell the truth, regardless of the cost. She is admittedly confessing to her friends sins they don't need to hear, just so she stays in the light. She is no longer allowing the powerful pull of peer approval to dictate her actions or view of herself. That alone is something precious she can take into adulthood, but it's been extracted from wasted years of self-inflicted pain.

Listening to her share her story, I was reminded of one of my favorite Ben Franklin anecdotes. I have long been a fan of his and the story of his sawdust pudding banquet.

Sometime after he set up his own newspaper, he began to receive feedback he was too honest in his editorials. Some of the greatest pressure he felt came from his advertisers, who threatened over time to stop running their ads if he continued to share his perspective when it wasn't in accordance with theirs.

Finally one evening Franklin invited them all to a banquet. When everyone arrived, they anticipated a feast—a dinner of appreciation for their advertising dollars. What they found instead set on the table were two dishes of cornmeal mush and a big pitcher of cold water. This kind of mush was eaten in this time period only by the very poor; and because it was yellow and coarse, it had earned the nickname "sawdust pudding."

Franklin ignored their stares and served everyone their bowl and then filled his own. The guests left their bowls untouched and gaped in amazement as Franklin finished his entire helping. Knowing they were all watching, he looked up from his meal and said quietly, "My friends, anyone who can live on sawdust pudding and cold water, as I can, does not need the approval of others."

HER STORY

Truth-telling is born out of being comfortable with who you are and then believing you have a right to what you think and a platform (or intimate environment) in which you can share that. It requires a level of confidence and an ability to exercise it in a variety of settings. This young woman might not see it yet, but I could tell from her desire to get the truth about her struggle accurately told that she was further down the healing road than she might imagine.

Our conversation began with the recognition that this is a story in flux. She asked me more than once to explain the premise of the project. I reassured her: "a testimony of the process, not the conclusion." She seemed pleased that I was curious about her whole story, not just her struggle with food. She wondered where to begin, and I stayed silent, knowing her mind was racing and not wanting to interrupt. Eating disorders are about hiding—those with this struggle make a lifestyle out of denial and secrecy. I was asking her to be counterintuitive.

She bravely began, "I was visiting a chiropractor about my bad back this week, and she was asking when my back issues began. 'You are young,' she commented, 'did you have an injury?'

"I sighed.

"In the last year and a half, I have committed to being honest about my relationship with food. I know healing lies in living in the light, so I opened up, 'I used to do hundreds, if not a thousand crunches a night . . . since junior high. It damaged my back as it was developing.'

> "Honesty creates connection. And connection is the antidote to hiding."

"What could she possibly say now? I braced myself for her advice or silence or judgment; I have seen it all. I have had some bad experiences with trained counselors and others with dear friends, so what could I expect someone like this to say?

"'I had an eating disorder as well,' she offered up quietly. She teared up, then I did too. We shared bits of our stories while she worked on my back. We formed a connection, and I left encouraged to keep being honest. Honesty creates connection. And connection is the antidote to hiding.

"One of the reasons I have had trouble starting any healing was that I couldn't admit my struggle was valid. It was never so serious that I was hospitalized, so I erroneously assumed I was still operating within a normal range. Years later, I know I was self-destructive, but because no one else seemed to notice, I excused my behavior for too long. Maybe someone could have/should have noticed enough

THEIR STORY ISN'T OVER

PRIOR to an eating disorder (which affects an estimated eleven-plus million Americans) there is a condition called "disordered eating." It's when a person's "attitude about food, weight and body size lead to very rigid eating and exercise habits that jeopardize one's health, happiness and safety" (nationaleatingdisorders .org). If you notice those behaviors in yourself or someone you love, it's critical to confront the situation before the symptoms escalate. Talking is the first step in "taking the teeth out of the tiger." He can still bite, but it won't hurt as much.

to get me some help, but I was a master at staying under the radar.

"I've realized that, more than self-control, God wants to bring restoration to the years I lost and to the brokenness of my thinking. I still waffle between condemning myself and surrendering it to the Lord. I am just trying to walk daily in the light, confessing thoughts as they arise and telling myself, as much as anyone else, the truth.

"I remember being young, as young as second grade, and already comparing myself to other girls. I was never overweight, but by third grade, I started thinking about dieting. I would compare myself with the popular girls, they seemed to have it easy—great clothes, all the boys had crushes on them. I always had nice clothes, but that wasn't our family's number-one priority. Attending a private school, though, there were families who apparently could have more than one priority.

"I look back now and feel hurt for that girl who was too young to defend herself from any enemy activity, seen or unseen. It swarmed around me and found this little foothold, this insecurity I was feeling, and it wedged itself in there to make camp. The lie that started as a whisper would become deafening: 'You are not good enough.'

"My first destructive step was taken at age eleven. Giving my mother the benefit of the doubt, it does seem incredulous that your young daughter would be stealing your diet pills. She never confronted me, so I assumed she was OK with it. And she continued to replace bottles she knew she'd never emptied. Last year, when I started down this path of healing and admission, I asked her why she didn't stop me. She swears she had no idea. I wonder, how could you not know? I complained of all the symptoms congruent with taking diet pills: my heart would race, I wouldn't eat, I was hyper and majorly over-exercising. She just didn't see it.

"I simply hoped it would make me super skinny and gain the attention of someone.

"I was born with a light-brown birthmark on my cheek and neck. My mom was always telling me that she thought I was beautiful,

> "The lie that started as a whisper would eventually become deafening: 'You are not good enough.'"

which went a long way in those years when my peers teased me. ('Rub in your makeup, why don't ya?') She was strong in words of affirmation, whether written or spoken. This felt so essential to me when I was young, when I drank up that message, wanting to believe it. It's curious to me that I always felt and still feel confident about my face, regardless of its color. Those words shored up that potential crack and it (unlike my body) was not a source of angst for me.

"The summer before seventh grade I went on a mission trip and at age twelve, I was by far the youngest. I looked up to one girl in particular, and she spent a lot of time with me, noticing me— something I hadn't always felt in a crowd before. I confessed one night to her about the pills and overexercising. I knew it was bad, and I wanted someone to confirm that, but she didn't have any sort of reaction. She didn't seem worried or concerned. Since part of my issue was seeking attention, I took her response and thought, *That's not good enough, I need to step it up a bit.*

> "Even today, I still can't understand why no one saw my self-destructive ways."

"I wonder now if maybe she shared that struggle? Maybe she didn't want me to feel guilty? didn't want to get involved? didn't understand it was a problem or what diet pills were? I don't know, but looking back, it definitely bumped me up to the next level.

"I started sports in junior high, which I loved since it meant I had a good excuse to exercise. I would come home from practice and my family would sit down to eat, but instead of joining them, I would go running. No one in my family ever said anything to me. No one asked me what I was eating, or saved me a plate. We had a very normal family—my parents were married, my sister was present at the table, we had a nice home, my dad was my best friend. Even today, I still can't understand why no one saw my self-destructive ways.

"My mom says she talked to my dad about it, and he said I was going through a phase and would be fine. So consequently, they didn't take me to a doctor, make me go to any counseling, or talk to my coach or school. We just didn't communicate about it.

"My issues stayed under the radar, which I both wanted and desperately didn't.

"From an adult perspective, I can see now the pain my parents had themselves. My mom struggles with depression. Admitting my downward spiral would have been another failure for her.

"In junior high, sensing a brewing storm, I would stay up making lists until 2 AM. How could I do things better? How could I be a better daughter? I thought I could fix anything if I was good enough, focused enough. At least I could make things easier for them.

"Meanwhile, I would lie when asked by anyone at school why I wasn't eating: 'I am fasting' or 'I had a big breakfast' or 'I'm not hungry.' Whatever it took for someone to be satisfied.

"As a sophomore in high school, I stopped playing basketball. I felt like God told me to lay it down, and the people in my life—my parents, coaches, and teammates—were confused and disappointed. I became depressed and missed the team. I struggled with doubt: Maybe I heard wrong? But I can see now what he was saving me from; it was becoming less about team camaraderie and more about an excuse to burn calories. An obsession.

"At the time though, I was just upset.

"It was during this year that I started making myself vomit. All my friends were so skinny and seemed to be able to eat anything. They looked great all the time. The only thing I could do to escape my negative thoughts (*I am not skinny. It's not fair. I am not good enough. . . .*) was run; it was my reprieve. I thought I was too fat to hang out with friends. I didn't want to go to church because I didn't have anything to wear. Looking back at pictures, in all reality I was tiny. But I was convinced I looked awful.

"I would do things to motivate myself to lose weight. I would make collages of skinny models. I would set goals: 'You have to lose this amount of weight in this amount of time' or 'OK, you can only eat five things' or 'You can only eat between 5 and 7 PM.'

"They were literally deals with myself to not take care of myself, and though it involved food, the roots were much deeper. If I broke one of my deals, then I would throw up. Trying to make something right with something worse. I dealt with so much shame and condemnation that I couldn't stick to any plan. I sometimes would wear a rubber band on my wrist to remind me not to eat, and I would smack it against my skin if I thought about food.

"I would look online and print out articles that actually supported girls in their anorexia. These articles were loaded with ideas of how to suppress hunger. They encouraged me to punish myself when I ate unnecessarily, but they called it 'discipline' (and thus, so did I).

"Complicating matters, I started to fast frequently. Even after I was coming out of all of this, I would still do it, but I knew I had impure motives. To this day, I have a hard time fasting.

"One week before my senior year in high school, while my mother and I were visiting family, my dad moved out of our home and out of his marriage. I was furious he didn't tell me of his plans; we were so close.

"When I saw him next, I noticed for the first time how much he was changing. He had lost fifty pounds, he had quit smoking, he was being healthy and feeling younger. And my mom didn't (or wouldn't) change with him. It was a volatile time for all of us, and she kicked me out of the house more than once, saying 'You love him more than me.'

"What can you say to that?

"Meanwhile, I was hopeful God (or I) could bring my family back together. There was a season when it looked like it might happen; my parents went on some dates. I was living with my dad in the apartment he rented and it was practically empty. He was having trouble creating a life away from us. That seemed like a good sign. He would break down, and I would play the counselor role—the mediator. I would listen and try to figure things out, from a perspective that didn't have all the facts or the maturity. Mediating for them is a pattern I am still trying to break from today.

"It was a really painful time, and although it looked like I was more than handling the situation, I know it made me ripe for seeking intimacy other places.

"My dad was thrilled with his new body and would weigh himself several times throughout the day. We would go on runs together and shoot hoops. Exercising was something we both enjoyed, and it became a way to connect. One memory from this season is burned into my mind. It was the day he wanted to compare our inner-thigh body fat to see who was in better shape. I felt so conflicted. I knew I didn't want to live like that (dieting, overexercising, vomiting, lying), but seeing his progress would only further my destructive behaviors. My dad was always who I had gravitated to, and now even he didn't always feel safe.

> "My dad was always who I had gravitated to, and now even he didn't always feel safe."

"I started dating this guy the winter after my dad left. We dated a year and a half, and it wasn't ever good. I compromised in everything. I lost a lot of weight when I was dating him. By then I was eighteen and could buy my own diet pills. He was older and in a position to move in order to be closer to me, and as a result, it became way too serious. He and I were meeting needs in each other in unhealthy ways.

"I went away to college for one semester, but I didn't want

to make any friends. I just wanted to be with my boyfriend. At this point I was turned off by all things religious. I had thought a Christian college was what I needed, but it repelled me even further. I would go to class and work out and continue losing weight. I would feel bad about myself and that drove me into the arms of my boyfriend, who made me feel better.

"Why couldn't someone see me?"

"Eventually I transferred to be closer to home and him. The night I moved back, we broke up. It was hard to face that rejection, and it made me vulnerable for when he decided he wanted me back. At that point our mutual obsession further escalated and became very intense, although it only lasted a couple more months.

"In the span of a week, my dad moved into our childhood home with his new girlfriend, my boyfriend broke up with me for good, my parents' divorce became final, and I faced emotionally what I had known cognitively for about a year—my sister was an alcoholic. Which, it turns out, everyone else had all known for years, but hadn't told me. They thought I wouldn't accept her, which was even more hurtful. Why didn't they trust me?

"We had all these struggles (eating disorder, depression, addiction, marital problems) and even though we shared a house, we had no idea what was going on with each other. Or if we suspected it on any level, we didn't communicate about it. My parents told me that as soon as they found out about my sister, they threw her into counseling and even that was hurtful to me. Here I was with an eating disorder. Why couldn't someone see me? Wasn't I worth some counseling dollars?

"Something that strikes me as I walk back over these memories is that I can't remember my dad ever expressing he thought I was beautiful. I remember him noticing if I had gained or lost weight. Once, when he came to pick me up from my dorm room for my birthday dinner, the very first thing he commented on was that I had lost weight. I was so pleased he noticed my hard work paying off. However, I was not pleased when a year and a half later he pointed out that I had gained weight.

"I am sure he is concerned about me and thinks he is helping. But no matter his intentions, every time he makes a comment about my weight, it feels like sabotage in the progress I'm making with this struggle. I take a step forward and one negative word from him sends me flying three steps back.

HIS STORY ISN'T OVER

I have known Miguel more than half his life. He is currently studying in our city's most prestigious university, earning a scholarship that covers 90 percent of the tuition. He is a man now, and I have watched his confidence grow as he is focusing more on what he is capable of and defining himself less on where he has been.

Miguel said, "I grew up never believing I would have a family. It was something others enjoyed, but wasn't a reality for me. I am currently studying healthcare and am hoping one day to be the Secretary of Health in Mexico."

"With the help of the Holy Spirit I am retraining my thinking on what it means and looks like to be beautiful. God is so much more concerned with my inner beauty: 'The LORD does not look at the things people look at. People look at the outward appearance, but the LORD looks at the heart' (1 Samuel 16:7). I want to lay down my perspective and exchange it for the Lord's, who offers me his perfect peace. I want to place focus and importance on the things God says are important and to live confidently, knowing what I have with him is truly beautiful and shines through.

"As a result of living in a home that looked one way on the outside but functioned without a lot of authenticity, today I value honesty. I have a high sensitivity toward others and can sense when someone is hiding something. I wish I hadn't honed it by doing it for so long myself. With my friends, I have become almost brutally honest, even confessing 'This is what I did today . . .' Living in the light has become my life mantra; I want it all out there—your stuff, my stuff. It's how I am stopping my cycle of self-destruction; it's how I truly see others and am seen.

> "I want it all out there— your stuff, my stuff."

"The biggest step forward for me in the last year is grasping the way God sees me and still loves me. I want to be a woman who sees others in the ways I longed to be seen. I want to love others as I longed to be loved.

"About a year and a half ago, I made the commitment to not buy another diet pill, so I put on forty-five pounds this year. I am choosing not to restrict myself externally while I work on what's going on internally. I am healthier than I have ever been in my life, and it's ironic to me how my family is noticing now that I need to lose weight. It's painful that they or others can't see the hard work I have put in—to talk through and forgive and unravel how this all started. It might not show up yet on my waistline, but that will come. I needed to start this year on the inside and not even dabble in counting calories, because honestly, that could still sidetrack me.

"From God's perspective, I think I have made huge leaps and progress. You can't see it, but I am trusting him in new ways. Dieting right now to lose this extra weight feels like it would be counterproductive. And I don't want anything to stop this healing and growth—not even the realization of my biggest fear, weight gain. I am hopeful in this journey. I am hopeful I will be healed. It takes patience to slow down my thinking long enough to decide if it's in line with God or my flesh, but that's the journey I am walking, knowing he is with me."

———————

Authenticity, intimacy with the Lord, a sensitivity to others, connection and community with friends, a desire to be in relationship with her family—this woman has more in her favor than she realizes. You hear her story and want to lean in to know *her* more, not just the story. You get the sense you could ask her anything and she'd tell you the truth. She seems to have a unique understanding of what's going on beneath the surface, and in spiritual terms, we call that discernment. It'll be another tool in her toolbox of life.

I even hear her mention her extra forty-five pounds and how she plans to shed it, and I envy her the process. I think it will be an ongoing conversation between her and her maker about her intense value, about how he wants to reward her with things other than food. I think it will be more about intimacy and less about fat grams, and that is simply stunning.

I finished the interview and wondered for what seemed like the hundredth time how often I have looked down the pew or around the circle or out in the crowd and have seen the outward indicators and not bothered looking beyond that. We have classes and committees and small groups full of us flawed human beings. We are rubbing elbows, but are we connecting?

It's complicated to enter into someone else's troubles. We have enough of our own, and the truth is, what can we do for them anyway? I am becoming convinced that, like Job's friends in the first part of his book, we can just sit there. Hear each other out. Listen to how we are growing or struggling in the midst of our circumstances. We all have wisdom earned in the heat of fire that can benefit the rest of the body of believers.

To know who we are in Christ's eyes and be content it's more than enough. To be able to live on the essentials, eating the proverbial sawdust pudding, and not worry about the approval of onlookers. That's the wisdom and the freedom I hear sprinkled throughout this young woman's story. It's still in process, but she has much to testify about already, and a world waiting to hear.

Look to the rock from which you were cut
and to the quarry from which you were hewn; . . .
The LORD will surely comfort Zion
and will look with compassion on all her ruins. . . .
Joy and gladness will be found in her,
thanksgiving and the sound of singing.

—ISAIAH 51:1-3

BETTY

Betty began, "My husband walked out on us when I was pregnant with our fourth child. I loved God with all my heart; so when he left me alone in the house, I prayed with faith and confidence, 'God, bring him back to us. Please.' I pleaded with the Lord, afraid somewhere in the back of my mind that the separation was his idea because maybe I loved my husband more than God. *Are you punishing me?* I was hoping for a miracle—that he would come back—and I was hoping the verses I was quoting from Scripture would sustain me in the meantime.

"I was constantly confronted with skeptics, people trying to bring me back to 'reality.' They wanted me to make plans for my life, prepare to deliver alone. Once in church, a friend said, 'You still believe in God after all of this and what he will do?' I responded immediately with a verse I had memorized, and shaking her head, she walked away. *Why doesn't anyone else believe?* I wondered.

"As time marched on, I accepted he wasn't coming back. I let go of that dream, but the problem was I couldn't grab on to any other

AFTER spending a week in January serving the orphan children in Monterrey, Cathy was hooked. She told me, "God grew my obsession into a passion and then into a calling over the initial month after returning home. However, God called Greg, my husband, in a very different manner."

"Cathy dropped not-so-subtle hints that she believed the Lord was calling us to serve on the mission field," Greg said. "I told her not-so-subtly, 'No, he's not. I'm a pastor, not a missionary.'" But still feeling the Lord's calling, she began praying.

Over the next several months, the Lord wrestled with Greg. "I was an unwilling participant in these wrestling matches. Then on Mother's Day morning, the Lord spoke into my thoughts as I walked to the pulpit: 'Greg, I want you in Mexico.' That was all I needed. God knows who we are—he meets us where we are and speaks to us in ways that convince us of his call. When I told Cathy after the service that I had heard from the Lord, she said it was the best Mother's Day gift she'd ever had!"

in its place. I was broken. I left my heart in the emotional ICU and focused on my children. I worked, I parented, I went to church. That was my whole life. We constantly had no money and I sold items door to door—needing a job where I could bring my kids along with me, needing money so we could eat.

"One day I remember we were almost out of food in the kitchen; I couldn't seem to sell anything, and I didn't have enough gas to cook anyway. I served the last of our meager options for dinner. There wasn't enough for all the kids to eat and me as well. The oldest noticed I didn't have a plate and asked, 'Aren't you hungry?' I told her no.

"But in truth I was.

"That night, my heart was breaking. Did God see us here struggling? I knew we had nothing for breakfast. What was I going to tell the children? It was late and I found myself deep in prayer over our situation. The phone rang. I answered it and immediately recognized the voice of my pastor as he asked, 'What do you need?'

"He said he and his wife prayed each night before bed for the congregation and he sensed a voice urging, 'Call Betty. Call Betty.' He explained this was why he didn't start out with pleasantries; he knew there was something going on. I shared with him our struggle. He and his wife arrived later that night with bags full of food for our family.

"*Oh Lord, you are listening.*

"I stayed several more years in this city.

"The deepest pit I ever fell into seemingly came from out of nowhere. We had settled into a routine of school, work, and church, and looking back, I don't know how it happened. It was like I was in a fog. The reality is, I became pregnant out of wedlock with my daughter, child number five. When it was happening, the fog continued and I didn't feel depressed, or even desperate. I was shocked and scared, but felt immediately the forgiveness of Christ. I kept looking at the cross and I knew he still loved me and forgave me.

"Did God see us here struggling?"

"But I couldn't forgive myself. I just couldn't forgive myself.

"Left with few options, I decided to move back home to Monterrey. I needed the extended family support I would receive there. It was hard to tell my family; some were worried my baby would be born sick because it was a product of sin. That reinforced my fears and shame. I didn't want to believe that, and so was relieved when my daughter was born perfectly healthy. I went to work on forgiving myself and redefining our family structure. We had a new city, a new baby sister, a new job, and hopefully, a new start.

"After a couple of years in my mom's house with my five children, my siblings told me it was time to leave. They were right—I needed to stand on my own feet. I knew what I was making as a social worker, but could I care for my five children and cover all the expenses and be everywhere I needed to be? I remembered the empty cabinets of my life before as a single mother. More so than ever, I was going to have to rely on God's faithfulness.

"We found a little house near the bus lines, so my kids could catch the public transportation easily after I had left for work in the morning. I would pray more than anything the Lord would capture their hearts. I kept thinking if they could love him as passionately as I did, then we would have all the riches we needed.

"More so than ever, I was going to have to rely on God's faithfulness."

"We had some setbacks. My fourth child, Brenda, had problems with her feet. It started with a misdiagnosis, and when the doctors were talking to me about all the possibilities, and the surgeries she would eventually need, I began to cry. Reaching up to touch my face, I realized I hadn't cried in years, since I last learned I was pregnant. I had been holding it together and holding it in for too long. Once I started, I couldn't stop.

"My children reminded me of the God promises I had taught them on many occasions. My prayers were being answered! They were learning to lean on a God not limited by paychecks, or physical illness, or any other setback. Brenda's medical journey was long and challenging, but we learned how to come together as a family and we saw God's provision in stunning ways.

"On many occasions, the oldest two children would ask me if I was ever going to get married. I wondered silently if any man would want the responsibility of five children, and I had resigned myself to the fact that probably no one would. I was OK with that answer. I never thought about men anymore. My life was work, the house, the Lord, and my kids. So I would jokingly answer, 'When I find an American who has bright-colored eyes, who is tall, and of course handsome, whose arms would cover me when he hugs me, then I will consider marriage.' They would start laughing and I would join them, sighing a little as my heart sank."

JIM

Jim started with his story. "God has always blessed me throughout my life. I don't feel like there was a time when I really had anything I couldn't bear. I enjoyed my two kids as they were growing up, but as they were both preparing to go into college, I realized I had made my life all about theirs. I was a divorced dad and so I poured much of my energy into their activities, their sports, and now I was left wondering if my business was going to be enough for me in this next stage of life. I began to imagine a future where I would have enough success that I could leave work for a couple of months a year to travel and serve in Mexico, at a mission base I had visited with my children's school a few times.

"I ran that idea past the directors and one of them challenged me to consider coming for a whole year. At this point, I still wanted to hold onto my house, my comfort, my security of the business, but enjoy the benefits of serving. The more I thought about it though, the more the idea of a year in Mexico seemed just what I needed.

"The challenging thought for me was, Would I give up everything for God? I look back now and realize it was when I gave it all up that he blessed me with so much more. But at that point, I still couldn't see very far ahead. Leaving the comforts of my life was a huge step for my faith.

"One of the hardest parts as I prepared for my trip was leaving behind my mother. She was a widow and had come to depend upon me. I struggled with whether or not it was the right thing to go. The morning I pulled out of the driveway, she prayed for this new adventure and what God had for me there. I told her I would be back and she promised to come and visit in Mexico.

"Heading south was in many ways a release of controlling any agenda I'd had in the past."

"We had no way of knowing then she would soon become sick with cancer. I have great peace she was able to see me here and meet my new 'family.' She loved how happy I was with this decision to follow God's new direction for my life.

"I learned that as I was completely trusting God with every detail, he took care of me in ways I couldn't have cared for myself. I came to Mexico surrendered—I had no illusions I would ever get married again. I didn't know what a year away from my business would do, and with my children out of the house, I didn't know if there would be anyone for me to share my life with anymore. Heading south was in many ways a release of controlling any agenda I'd had in the past.

"It wasn't long after I arrived when a mutual friend introduced me to Betty. I was immediately drawn to her, and I wrestled with whether it was me who was drawn to her or God who was leading us together. I didn't want to get off track by following my own selfish desires. I prayed, *God, if this is of you, make it clear!* But I was falling in love fast and desperate to know if God would bless it. There

Jim and Betty outside their home in Mexico, 2011.

was a season of inner turmoil, then a peace—I honestly felt like God had given her to me."

JIM AND BETTY

Betty chimed in, "I fell in love with Jim right away. Even before we could totally understand each other, I watched him with people and was attracted to his easy, servant-like nature. But I couldn't imagine anyone paying attention to me. I could sense him responding to me, seeking me out, listening to me, and I felt comfortable with him right away. My reaction to him was almost something spiritual. God was uniting us and I could feel it. Many people said, 'It won't last. What do they have in common?' But we knew how our stories were intertwining. We could feel it and talked about how God was with us.

"For me, it was (and still is) like living in a dream. All my life I had wanted to work for God. I knew I could always do more. I longed to spend my days in ministry. Jim would take me on dates, not to fancy restaurants, but to the orphanage or the squatters' villages where his ministry worked. I was thrilled, and kept asking the Lord if this was real. Does this man, whose eyes are blue, who is tall and has strong arms, this man I asked you for—does he really love you and want to spend his days working for you? And is it my imagination he wants me to be beside him?"

> "We marvel today at how we couldn't do life without the other."

Jim continued, "I knew that Betty would be a helpmate—a person I could share more than my life with, I could share my passion for serving. I asked her to marry me one beautiful summer night on a boat near my home. I felt that evening the rain of God's blessings fall on us.

"We had both been through so much and it made us appreciate each other all the more. There was no doubt he was in this. It felt good to know it was not just him helping *me* make something work of my own design, but instead it was him sharing with me a plan *he* had written for us both. We marvel today at how we couldn't do life without the other. We are intertwined in every sense—our family, our work, our hearts. I couldn't do life without her. I let go of what now seems inconsequential to gain a dream I had forgotten I had."

Betty finished out their story. "We were seated at our wedding and one of the speakers said, 'If you know Jim and Betty, you know either one of them would give you the shirt off their back. It will be fun to watch what God will do with a couple like this.' I think now I hardly heard him talk. I was looking at my children, and their joy on this day seeing God answer the prayers of their mother. I was wondering what changes were ahead; how much more I was going to get to know this man God had given me. I caught his eye and I knew he felt like I did—this day was a dream come true for us."

———————

I noticed they moved closer together on the couch as our time together passed. It's been three years since their wedding and they still look like newlyweds to me. They minister together on our staff to a children's home and a squatters' village. In the aftermath of our city's devastating hurricane this past summer, they went to work daily in the parts of the community most impacted by the storm. I overheard them share their testimony, speaking to men and women and children about how God uses the storms of our lives to reveal himself to us and how he will restore that which has been broken.

THEIR STORY ISN'T OVER

THESE beautiful girls share a common heritage. They have all been expelled from their villages because both their parents have died and in the minds of fellow villagers, they are "cursed." I heard them sing one afternoon a sweet song, thanking the Lord for what he has provided them. They were an example to me that day in asking the same question with the right attitude, not "Why me, Lord?" (Why the deaths? Why the expulsion?) but "Why me, Lord?" (Why did you pick me up and set me upon the rock? Why didn't you leave me to die?)

Jim talked of how God uses hardships to refine us and shape our lives. Betty spoke about the faith muscle we can exercise and the intimacy we can have with Jesus when he is all we have.

Relentless hope.

Hope in a God who never lifts his pen from the story of our

lives. Who watches all the chapters, both the good and the hard, and cheers us to press on—to believe in what's to come, to use what we have grown through, to know it's not over yet.

Jim and Betty are extracting the precious from the worthless. They are using the hard parts of their story to relate to others who are struggling. They are watching God use their life experiences to his glory. Their wedding was a billboard for a God who redeems.

I hear Betty talking frequently to young, single mothers, who are battling with provision and juggling more responsibilities than possible, and encouraging them to trust God for each day. I watch Jim sharing from experience the joy he has found on the other side of release. They are inspiring, but we would miss the point if we were inspired by them alone. The inspiration is a reflection of a God who never tires of walking us home.

> The LORD will surely comfort Zion
> and will look with compassion on all her ruins;
> he will make her deserts like Eden,
> her wastelands like the garden of the LORD.
> Joy and gladness will be found in her,
> thanksgiving and the sound of singing.

These promises were penned a couple thousand years before Jim met Betty. But the Lord who spoke them is still the same. He is in the business of redemption. Sometimes the redeeming has its own timeline, and we grow impatient. Sometimes a dream has to die for another to be accepted. Sometimes it takes a season in the desert to appreciate the sight of water.

11

REAL ESTATE IN THE LAND
OF NO NEAT ANSWERS

There I will give her back her vineyards,
and will make the Valley of Achor a door of hope.

—HOSEA 2:15

When we sense opposition, it's our tendency to strike a defensive pose. That is our instinct for self-preservation—our way of ensuring that we will be safe from the impending strike. Jesus teaches us a different pose. "If your enemy is hungry, give him food to eat; if he is thirsty, give him water to drink. In doing this, you will heap burning coals on his head, and the LORD will reward you" (Proverbs 25:21, 22).

> When we sense opposition, it's our tendency to strike a defensive pose.

I never understood this passage. Paul quoted it again in Romans. It's written as a strategy—to win over the enemy, not conquer him. And until recently, I wondered, how again do burning coals help that?

One spring I taught in a church during a series they were doing on covenants. I was assigned the Abrahamic covenant, and I studied extensively Genesis 15. God sealed his promise to Abraham (for all the descendants like stars in the sky) with a blood path covenant, a common practice in those days between two parties. They would cut the animal or animals to be sacrificed in half, then allow the blood to pool together in a path, which both parties would walk through. This would be a signal to their families that if they broke the agreement they had just made, the offending party had permission to hold them accountable even to the point of bloodshed.

When God instructed Abraham to create a blood path covenant, and to find the animals and split them, I wonder what Abraham was thinking. He knew how he could walk through the covenant, but how would God walk the blood path?

God moved through the path in something theologians call a *theophany*, or the appearance of God, and used a smoking firepot to represent his presence. It makes for some fascinating reading and sealed a promise that Abraham would stand on through all the coming events in his life. The presence of God does that—it stays with you. It motivated Abraham to take risks, love others, and believe.

Bible teacher Ray Vanderlaan connected for me the story of Abraham I had studied and the forementioned passage about enemies and burning coals. He said that once we know that a smoking firepot—or in other words, some burning coals—represented God's presence, it makes sense we are directed to love our enemies in ways they don't deserve, and that by doing so, we bring God's presence into their lives. That pose is far more strategic than fending off incoming arrows; it places us in a position behind the cross. Our hope is that by exposing our opposition to burning coals, they would come to understand God's love for them to the point that they take risks, love others, and believe.

———————

It's a unique person who can live in the space between the events unfolding in his life and the emotions that threaten to overwhelm as a result of those events. It was while I was listening to my friend, who lives in that space, share his heartbreaking story with me, that I felt compelled to write this book. He told me he hasn't found a platform to share his story of how God is coming through for him. The church, he claims, seems more interested in spotlighting stories where the diagnosis was reversed, the marriage restored, or the baby healed.

His story isn't over yet, but it's been in a long, dark chapter. Yet, if you talk to him, you can hear odd notes of a relentless kind of hope, a hope in Jesus, the person, more than hope-it-will-all-get-worked-out-in-the-end, or hope in some doctrine. It's a hope marked by a strong voice of conviction, an intense tenderness, a lot of wisdom, and a palpable compassion for his children. It may not be a traditional "testimony," but there are volumes going on to testify about.

> The presence of God does that—it stays with you.

THE WILDERNESS

He started with skepticism—unsure if I would be open to hear him share his pain as he has struggled himself to get his head and heart around it. Many, he said, are willing to say hello and ask how he's doing, but few are willing to patiently sit while he shares. Often the response is "If you need anything let me know," or "Give me a call sometime."

We met several times, as he unraveled his heartbreaking story. I have known him more than a decade and a half and I wonder, like many others, *How did this happen?*

He looked at me across the table, almost daring me not to wiggle in discomfort. Without breaking eye contact, he began, "The first year of our marriage was fraught with more difficulties than either

THEIR STORY ISN'T OVER

THIS visiting team to our site in Mexico is working hard to shape some rebar (short for reinforcing bar). Over and over again, I have seen that when a group of people work toward a common goal, they experience the residual benefit of drawing together and gaining new perspective. The work ends up blessing both the receiver and the giver.

God is remarkably multifaceted like that. The fastest way to experience community (and expel loneliness or gain new perspective or appreciation) is to serve. My own questions these days have been: For whose benefit am I working? Who am I coming alongside? It's an awful lot of work to bend the metaphorical rebar; I sure want it to count for more than just the moment.

of us had anticipated. In the midst of our church splitting and needing to find a new church home, a significant career change for me, our first baby, and struggles with our respective families, we found ourselves in need of counseling. We wanted to be proactive in learning how to connect better as husband and wife. At this point, we knew we were absorbing more stress than we could handle in a healthy way, and we were having trouble communicating. We both hoped counseling would give us tools to navigate this difficult foundational season.

"We were led to an elder Christian to help counsel us through those formative years of our marriage—a man with years of experience in helping others like ourselves. He was a charismatic figure to us, knowledgeable in the Scriptures, emphatic in his points, and able to help us change how we thought about our circumstances, ourselves, and our very own beliefs. He was able to help develop in us a deeper path of communication that we so desperately needed.

"Through our time together we found a friendship growing

around the energies and passions that arose from the concepts we discussed. Our circle of counseling grew to take in other close friends we felt safe with, who would also help shape the ideas we discussed.

"Over time, however, I began to feel troubled as I noticed a dynamic developing between this man and my wife. I began to feel a distance form between my wife and me, and I had to believe that this man was also sensing this distance between us, and the energy that was building between him and her. In fact, it looked to me like he was encouraging it.

"At one point I confronted him about what I perceived were feelings he had toward her ('Do you have romantic feelings for my wife?'), and inappropriate comments that I didn't appreciate him making. I felt bold, panicked, entitled to my questions.

"*What was going on?*

"He assured me there were no inappropriate feelings and apologized for his off-color remarks."

"The next chapter in my story is a blur. I was devastated to learn some time later that the feelings between the two of them had escalated into a full-blown affair. I confronted both of them and told them to end it, but they both refused. It was like an arrow piercing my heart when they told me that they were deeply in love and had to have each other.

"I honestly didn't know what to do.

"I ceased all contact with the man and his family while my wife and I remained together for a season. I hoped and prayed they would come to their senses and end the affair. I still loved her, and believed in fighting for our family, for us. Instead, the affair deepened, and the two became more devious in how they attempted to hide it from their spouses.

"There were excruciatingly painful nights when the kids would sit up, not willing to go to bed until their mom came home (from being out with him). I would sit beside them, not sure how to comfort them while I was in so much pain myself.

"The situation reached a boiling point. My wife moved out, saying she could no longer live with me. I was devastated. I had spent months praying and reading Scripture to gain direction, clarity, and even hope.

"*God, what do I do? Do I let her go? Do I chase after her? Is there hope for the marriage? Do I divorce her? What about the kids?*

"I felt like I had a biblical and moral foundation for pursuing the divorce, but the idea of it was still so frightening, so painful.

> "The hurting should never have to be the ones to reach out."

"*God, is there any other option?*

"For the first time in years, I found myself alone in a house I had dreamed of being a home for my family. I would sit alone and cry out in prayer, 'God, is this how you answer my prayers? She's gone! How can this get any worse?'

"A few months later my wife shared with me she was pregnant with his child.

"How can it still surprise me? the betrayal?

"That singular event seemed to embody all my deepest pains and fears. The consequences to her actions now felt irreversible. After that conversation all that I had come to believe about myself, my faith, and my perspective of God and his love toward me were called into question. A history of perceived betrayals, rejections, insults, and injuries going back all the way to my childhood began rolling through my mind, and with it a growing sense that I was not being spared once again from the enemy's wounding.

"God, where is the shelter under your wing you promised your loved ones? Where is your protection?"

———————

He continued, "Our friends and family have had varied reactions; some people have chosen to give me space, thinking it's easier (on who? me or them?). It can still sting—thinking about those in the church who knew about the affair, but never talked to us about it.

"After my wife moved out and I hadn't heard from some people in a while, I decided to approach them to see if, in the ugliness of dealing with my pain, I had offended them or driven them away. (The hurting should never have to be the ones to reach out in such situations, however. It almost always costs more emotional energy than we have most days.) Their response: 'No, not at all, we just thought you needed some space.' On one such occasion I spoke boldly in reply. 'What I need is companionship. I have plenty of space and periods where I am alone. That's when it's the hardest.'

"We hung up, and I wondered if things would change. Would I have to continue to be the one to call for help, to ask for a listening ear, when most days I could barely get out of bed? What really hurt is that I'm sure there were some who—in their desire to rescue the prodigal, the wayward one—had distanced themselves from me on purpose in order to maintain a relationship with her."

———————

I paused my interviewer mode to ask him pleadingly what he wanted. We as a church know a thing or two about going after those who are running away. We pursue, love unconditionally, speak truth, and pray. But what would he teach us about loving those who are wounded? about going after the victims, those who are suffering?

He told me that, while reading the book of Job, one aspect of that story that most impressed him was the response of Job's three friends when they heard of his plight: they got together, formed a plan, left their other responsibilities, and then sat in silence for seven days, mourning with Job. Not a word was spoken until Job himself spoke.

> "Pain shaped how I prayed."

"Beth," he said, "isn't that one of the qualities we find most moving about God—no matter where we are in life, he will meet and sit with us there? To be honest, that's what I find most helpful. It's not so much those who try to offer advice or counsel, or who try to suggest passages of Scripture, as if my thinking or theology needs to be redirected. For me it feels as if they're more concerned about what *they* should say—that they somehow need to be God's defender or advocate, rather than simply hearing my heart.

"The most helpful people to me are those who are willing to count the cost of stepping into the experience of someone in deep pain and who allow themselves to offer what truly matters in that moment—a heart willing to share the pain.

"At times it feels like a game of spiritual horseshoes—rather than get close to the sufferer and enter into his pain, we outsiders stand at a distance and toss what we think are little nuggets of truth or encouragement. We feel like we've done our job as a brother or sister in Christ when we toss that 'spiritual ringer,' we utter what we feel 'God has led' us to say, but still do not enter into the other person's experience.

A snapshot of a land of no neat answers.

"To the recipient however, it just feels like we have cast something heavy toward his head. We leave the person still feeling alone in his pain. And I don't doubt in those moments that God does speak or is speaking through his body of believers. But those words to me feel so much more palatable when they're accompanied by a merciful heart that is not easily offended by the words and emotions of the sufferer, and when they're spoken with an understanding that only comes with a heart engaged over time—not just in the moment."

———

His story resumed, "Things reached a crescendo of sorts when the day arrived for the child's birth and the introduction of him to our children. Prior to his birth our children did not know the child was not mine, nor even up to that point did they have any knowledge of the affair. It was then that she had to communicate to them the truth, the truth regarding the baby and where her heart was.

"After that I had to have conversations with my children I had never in my life dreamed of having. Hearing the pain and confusion in their voices when they wondered about what their future would look like, about stepparents and separate homes, was like having a knife stabbed into my heart.

"At that time I felt probably the most paradoxical moments I had ever had in my walk of faith—I had a deep burning anger toward God for what he had allowed to happen, but also a peace and strength underneath it all holding me up and giving me words to speak when they felt so hard to come by.

"Through those years I came to a pivotal point in my walk, a crisis of faith. Pain shaped how I prayed. In the beginning it was a lot of 'God, do this; God, do that.' Then came, 'Screw it, God, you are not playing by my rules—doesn't even seem like you are playing by your rules. She is obviously in sin, and you are not doing a d*#n thing!'

"It felt pointless to pray, so I stopped for a time, my last words being, 'If you stop talking, then I will too.'

"It was in silence that God changed my perspective. I had to stop praying the 'God, do this' prayers and begin praying the 'God, where are you?' prayers. Not from a sense of despondency, of despair, but a sincere request—like a child calling out to a parent. And not in the sense that I couldn't see God, and not in the sense that he'd abandoned me. Instead, it was me confessing: 'God, you created the universe and have set everything in its place. It was your will to perfect obedience in your son through suffering, and you have desired the same for me. I can't fight you anymore, and over the years I've hurt the people closest to me, those I care the most

> "If God is in my wilderness, then I will be there too."

about, out of my fears and need to control. The path before me is wrought with pain, but I know you've already walked it, and you will take me to where my healing is.'

"To step back and pray 'God, I'm so deeply wounded and scarred I can't even see straight and know what to pray anymore' was one of the most terrifying and freeing moments for me. *What if God doesn't come through for me? What if I do let go of my sense of control? Will I allow myself to discover what God truly does feel toward me and the lengths he'll go to in order to reveal himself to me?*

"I don't want to be pulled toward the wilderness; I much prefer the land of milk and honey, of ease and comfort, of prosperity. But the truth is, I just want to be there—I want to be there with him, wherever 'there' is. In Hosea 2, God speaks about winning his people back. 'I am now going to allure her; I will lead her into the wilderness and speak tenderly to her. There

OUR STORY ISN'T OVER

I recently went bungee jumping with some friends off a mountain in Mexico. I trash-talked my way all the way there and through the harness fitting and during the long walk out to the end of the plank. Then . . . I found myself looking down on all the tree tops and realized (a little late) how counterintuitive bungee jumping is. It's ridiculous really (although I have to admit I have done it more than once). Out on the end however, I felt something extraordinarily spiritual as I started talking to, bargaining with, and begging God.

I thought an inordinate amount of time about my next step.

How often do I walk (in this direction or that one) without thinking? I often skip along paths of my own making, feeling full of pride at where I am heading, forgetting completely that "the LORD determines our steps" (Proverbs 16:9, *NLT*). Lord, forgive me!

I will give her back her vineyards, and will make the Valley of Achor [Trouble] a door of hope' (vv. 14, 15).

"If God is in my wilderness, then I will be there too."

———————

"I am taking ownership of my part these days. I have made a decision to stop the language of shame and condemnation with her and about her. I did spend a lot of time initially thinking and praying about what I could do to save her/change her/rescue her. But as I forcibly have time alone now, I choose to think and listen and be still. And I ask questions of myself instead: *Who am I? What do I really believe? How do I feel about God? And what are his feelings toward me? Why do I struggle so deeply to believe in my heart he truly loves me?*

"Every heart has a story associated with it that is filled with triumphs and tragedies, joys and pains."

"I know what the Word says—I've been a student of the Bible for years. So I wanted to figure out what is at the core of this disconnect for me—why I could know God so loved the world he sent his only Son and yet tend to gravitate toward a response of 'That's all well and good, but to feel loved I need something else.' I had created a sense in myself that I'm really not worthy of love, and my desires really don't matter to others. So when something happened that touched on my sense of unworthiness, and especially something of this scale, I felt the enemy standing in the background smirking: 'You will never be free of this bondage. You will never measure up. You really don't matter.' It is an awareness of this fear that I've come now to take ownership of.

"The shift has happened, and it feels a little like liberty. I can still feel an ache for us both—I know her well enough to know how she is struggling through her choices. She has a history that led to this season and this was just a later, unfortunate chapter in her story.

"For that reason, amidst some controversy, I can honestly say that, with her sincere repentance, I would take her back into my life. I wonder if she'll ever come back to be the person I once knew her to be, but if she did return, I believe I would rejoice. And with that is a willingness now to repent of my own issues, to not take ownership of her or anyone else's choices, to not blame myself, but to step back and see her heart and mine as both valuable and precious to God. To see that every heart has a story associated with it that is filled with triumphs and tragedies, joys and pains. And every one of those stories needs to be shared and heard."

AFTER THE SHIFT

"The storm hasn't passed by any means, but I am managing my anxiety with more experience now than I did a couple years back. I think all anxiety is rooted in unspoken secrets, and I am talking more now, so there aren't many secrets left. I am using language that reflects Jesus' teaching and truthfulness.

"I tell my kids when I am hurting, and I allow them the same privilege. Lately, the greatest conversations of the heart I've had with my children have tended to occur after emotional conflict. We are developing a deep trust in relationships where there is a freedom to express our feelings, but also an ability to reign in those feelings. In the calm that follows, a stream flows carrying our words deep into each other.

"Last week, during our family devotions, I brought the kids into my room and we all climbed up onto my bed. I read them the verses about Jesus washing the feet of his disciples. I then, one by one, prayed the truths I see in them and washed their feet. I said some prayers out loud; I wanted them to hear how I talk to God and what qualities I have seen developed in them. And I prayed some pleas silently.

"I prayed for their future, wanting them to be protected as much as possible. I prayed for their relationships with Jesus, that they would know him as one who would never fail them. I prayed our experience would develop in them a greater faith and capacity for love. And I prayed for our family, that we would stand as a testimony of a family marked by our time spent with him.

"It has been a joy to see in this time my oldest children give their hearts to Jesus and take hold of their faith. In some ways I envy them for the pain that they have felt through all of this. As a result, they will develop a deeper sense of compassion, mercy, and faith than I had as a child. Jesus once said that 'whoever has been forgiven little loves little' (Luke 7:47), and the one who's been forgiven much loves much.

"This experience is changing me. The alone times I feared so much before the separation have instead become times of intense reflection and soul searching. There are no more excuses, no more procrastination—I am either going to work out my salvation with fear and trembling, or go through life trying to numb myself or be 'delivered' from the pain and suffering that accompanies our time here. I've been deeply unnerved by the things God has revealed to me about me. But like the pain that comes with having to break a bone to reset it properly, it has all been for good.

"I have no idea how my story will end or what that good ending will look like. I find myself having to let go daily of how I think God should define that ending. I'm learning to trust whatever ending he writes will be good. I know my citizenship is in Heaven, and there's an eternal reward being stored up for me there. But I also have to believe I'm living in that eternity now, and what I've come to find is the good I think God desires for me aren't good gifts in the earthly sense—what we call blessings. His good for me is the giver himself. If I have him, what else is there?

"What I'm endeavoring to be is less concerned about how I finish the race and more conscious of how I live in the moment, aware of God's deep abiding presence in me. If I'm living in that moment-by-moment awareness, won't the end work itself out as intended? Rather than worry about a tomorrow that hasn't happened, I am working to embrace now and whatever feeling each moment brings.

"Jesus was never afraid to feel the full depth of any emotion. He was never afraid his feelings would overwhelm him—he welcomed them and lived them out before others. The Jesus who was so deeply moved to cry at the tomb of Lazarus with his fam-

> "I have no idea how my story will end or what that good ending will look like."

ily, and who raised him from the dead, is the same Jesus who was so deeply moved at the temple to take the time to fashion a whip and drive people out. In both events there was no holding back of emotions, there was no sin, there was no shame. He was still Jesus. There's a proper way of expressing those feelings—it's like a fire. Built in a fireplace it can provide warmth; outside the fireplace it can burn a house down. Exploring my feelings, my fire, and for a time allowing them to be has helped develop a greater awareness of God's feelings toward me.

"And I've deeply needed that awareness for a long time."

He paused, and I stared.

His head is still above the water. He is, in some sense, beyond just surviving and is thriving. How is that possible?

Relentless hope.

Not hope in her, or hope in a fairy-tale ending, but hope in a God that is more real to him with each passing minute.

I hugged him and decided not to say too much. I affirmed him as a man, communicating how much I respected his vulnerability and decision to become even more so dependent on Jesus, instead of falsely standing on his own. I told him I was jealous of his relationship with the Lord, which seems so organic.

He probably felt spent after our time together, but seemed battle-ready. He was drawing from a well that will never go dry and that has been tested on all the days his own strength was gone. Those days and that well have made him a better father, I suspect, a better friend, a better listener, and a better man. Although I doubt he quite realizes it yet.

I drove away, immediately craving an intimate session with Jesus. I wanted to process with him what I saw in my friend, what I envied in him—real estate in the land of no neat answers.

I refuse to put a bow or even an explanation on his circumstances.

I still struggle myself with wanting to believe God has a plan for my life, but all the while demanding my free will. *Let it go!* I plead with myself. Make it for a moment more about the maker than his message for me. Make it more about connection and less about results.

Forgive me, Lord. Teach me to hear you, to be content above all else with dwelling in you—even if that means living in the wilderness. Reveal more of yourself to my friend tonight and to his children, and to his wife—and let that be enough. Amen.

12

HE WILL WARN US OF WRONG TURNS (AND WHITE PICKUPS AND BAD FIANCÉS)

*Elisha, the prophet who is in Israel, tells the king of Israel
the very words you speak in your bedroom.*

—2 KINGS 6:12

I was in Israel this past year, traveling with Bible teacher Ray Vanderlaan and some friends through the country, learning in Technicolor about God's text. Ray isn't the kind of guide who drones on and on about facts that collect dust in a notebook you never open. He is much more Indiana Jones than tour guide Barbie. This point was proven on a hot day when we were traveling to Tiberius. He spotted far off in the hills a shepherd boy and his flocks of sheep and goats. Sensing a teachable moment, he stopped our bus and led us all on a challenging boulder field hike, straight up into the hot, Middle Eastern sunshine.

When we got to the summit, we sat and watched the animals for a minute. The shepherd, in his early teens, used only his voice and was constantly talking to the herd. The sheep formed completely straight lines and followed him so tightly, that if one stopped, they all bumped into the rear of the one in front of them. He stopped frequently, and from my vantage point, I could see the sheep reach down between the rocks and grab tufts of hidden grass. Then ten or twenty steps later, the process was repeated.

Ray began to teach. "When the shepherd David penned Psalm

> "Worry is eating tomorrow's problems in today's pasture."

23, he was not waist deep in alfalfa grass. When he writes about being led to green pastures, he has in his mind's eye the careful leading to the next mouthful of grass the sheep need to survive. Look around you—this is the green pasture of David's land. When we find ourselves hungry, we would do far better to be so close to the Shepherd that we hear when he stops and points out the next mouthful of grass we need."

We sat quietly and listened, each pondering what it means to rethink a theology that says we deserve belly-deep alfalfa. What it means to not demand it or whine in its absence, but to be grateful for the nourishment in the moment. Ray interrupted my thoughts with a rabbinic quote that struck me funny: "Worry is eating tomorrow's problems in today's pasture." I looked around—there wasn't enough grass for today and tomorrow. There was hardly enough for today it seemed, and yet the sheep were fine.

Then I saw the goats, who had been meanwhile roaming wherever they chose. They were up and down, on the edges of cliffs, not getting near the nourishment the sheep were. They were wild, and some were running in front of the shepherd while others were falling far behind.

In Matthew 25:31-46, we find the story Jesus told about the sheep and goats:

> When the Son of Man comes in his glory, and all the angels with him, he will sit on his glorious throne. All the nations will be gathered before him, and he will separate the people one

from another as a shepherd separates the sheep from the goats. He will put the sheep on his right and the goats on his left.

Then the King will say to those on his right, "Come, you who are blessed by my Father; take your inheritance, the kingdom prepared for you since the creation of the world. For I was hungry and you gave me something to eat, I was thirsty and you gave me something to drink, I was a stranger and you invited me in, I needed clothes and you clothed me, I was sick and you looked after me, I was in prison and you came to visit me."

Then the righteous will answer him, "Lord, when did we see you hungry and feed you, or thirsty and give you something to drink? When did we see you a stranger and invite you in, or needing clothes and clothe you? When did we see you sick or in prison and go to visit you?"

The King will reply, "Truly I tell you, whatever you did for one of the least of these brothers and sisters of mine, you did for me."

Then he will say to those on his left, "Depart from me, you who are cursed, into the eternal fire prepared for the devil and his angels. For I was hungry and you gave me nothing to eat, I was thirsty and you gave me nothing to drink, I was a stranger and you did not invite me in, I needed clothes and you did not clothe me, I was sick and in prison and you did not look after me."

They also will answer, "Lord, when did we see you hungry or thirsty or a stranger or needing clothes or sick or in prison, and did not help you?"

He will reply, "Truly I tell you, whatever you did not do for one of the least of these, you did not do for me."

Then they will go away to eternal punishment, but the righteous to eternal life.

Sheep follow, they listen, they eat what is provided, they stay in a line—all things I have historically struggled in. Goats, they are in it for themselves, following impulses instead of others. They are sure their path is right, even when it means constant backtracking and jockeying.

Lord, I want to be a girl who is in line with your voice, who sees the sick or the hungry and isn't in the journey only for herself. It's so tempting to be swayed by voices in our culture that tell you it's all about you and your path to self-satisfaction. It's about your fulfillment, your dreams, your best life, your making it your own way. It sounds so tempting, so alluring to make a path of my own creation, but watching the flock from the top of the hill, the goats just looked silly. They seemed flighty and frankly, dumb for not listening to the one person who could help them avoid the rock spills and find the nourishment they needed to survive.

I get it, Lord, I see it, I feel it, I hear you. Don't give up on me, this girl is gonna get it yet!

WHITE PICKUPS

"Ahh!!!!"

I sat straight up in bed, shaking, trying to orient myself in the room. Once I was awake enough to realize where I was, I jumped out of bed and ran to my son Joshua's room. There he was sleeping safe in his bed.

I turned and walked slowly down the hall, still rattled by the memories of my dream. Unable to settle down enough to return to sleep, I woke up Todd to tell him I had dreamt a man in a white pickup truck had kidnapped Joshua. It was so vivid it was hard to shake. To his credit, he woke up enough for us to pray and then fell back asleep, although I tossed around the rest of the night.

The next morning as everyone was coming over to begin the work day, one of our staff members, Gabriel, pulled Todd aside. "I had a dream last night, and I don't know, this feels weird, but I wanted to tell you about it—it was so real. A man in a white truck came onto the property and, well . . . he kidnapped Joshua."

Todd didn't hear the rest, as holy alarms went off in him and he came to find me (and Joshua). We didn't really know what to think; we were just very concerned.

HIS STORY ISN'T OVER

SEBASTIAN grew up thinking he would never be anyone important in life—that no one knew or cared about what he had to say or to offer. But his outlook has changed. "Today, I have a better understanding of who I am in Christ and who I am as a man, and that has translated into the hope that I am someone who can be used by God. My current dream as a culinary student is to be a chef who travels internationally. I wonder what I will find out there."

Later that day we were sharing the dreams with another friend, asking him what he thought they meant, and he showed us the following passage in 2 Kings 6:8-12 (*The Message*):

One time when the king of Aram was at war with Israel, after consulting with his officers, he said, "At such and such a place I want an ambush set."

The Holy Man sent a message to the king of Israel: "Watch out when you're passing this place, because Aram has set an ambush there."

So the king of Israel sent word concerning the place of which the Holy Man had warned him. This kind of thing happened all the time.

The king of Aram was furious over all this. He called his officers together and said, "Tell me, who is leaking information to the king of Israel? Who is the spy in our ranks?"

But one of his men said, "No, my master, dear king. It's not any of us. It's Elisha the prophet in Israel. He tells the king of Israel everything you say, even what you whisper in your bedroom."

> It felt like God was allowing us to hear the whisperings of the enemy camp.

It felt like God was allowing us to hear the whisperings of the enemy camp, the plans we shouldn't have known about. I don't know for sure, but I believe the enemy was preparing to ambush our family, and God saw it fit to thwart that plan. It was a warning, and one we took seriously to pray and protect our son. We still take extra precautions and are more aware of other people than I am sure we would have been otherwise. Even remembering this story now, years later, I feel tempted to shake my fist and ask, Why don't we always get that kind of luxury? to know the movements of the enemy before they happen?

Although in this case the warning was very personal, we already know what is in his playbook. The one who opposes us will try and tempt us with lust and greed and anger and fear and pride. He will wrap himself around ideas of self-justification, self-righteousness, self-gratification, self-regard. He will hide seamlessly inside self-destruction, self-deception, self-glorification, self-motivation, self-loathing, and self-pity. Such an intense focus on self, even in seemingly healthy ways can lead to a lost focus on the Lord. He has used the same tricks since the beginning of time; they should be obvious now from far off. Why can they still so easily sidetrack me?

I have known the Lord for more than three decades. You'd think that would mean I'm gaining ground in wisdom and insight. The truth is, I have today more questions than answers. I understand less, but am confident of more. I have a stronger faith muscle to be OK with what I don't always know, but I refuse to make up an excuse for God when I don't understand his actions.

Why did he seem to warn me this time, but not someone else another?

When I began to solicit stories on how ordinary people heard God through extraordinary circumstances, I had my inbox and my ear filled with angel sightings, quiet promptings, perfectly timed sermons, lost notes found, and the list goes on and on. We see God when we look for him, in a number of ways. And whether they all are him intervening or some are just coincidences, I don't know. But I never get tired of our yearning to understand. I do believe though, when we seek him, we will find him, and my friend Julie's story teaches us just that.

SUBWAY LADY

She started, "I was born the youngest of ten children. I attended Catholic school and was a very happy child who loved our lively

HER STORY ISN'T OVER

ONE of my favorite people to spend time with is our foster daughter, Lupita. Having lived in either a children's home or a foster home her whole life, she is a spitfire of joy and premature wisdom. She wanted to share in her own words what life has taught her thus far. "I am dreaming about a future where the battle isn't as great as it has been. Where my children don't experience some of what I have had to experience. I believe God has blessed me and ultimately, has a plan for me, so I trust in him daily. I have learned many things in my fifteen years, but mainly that God is the only one who has control and that he is always with me, never letting me go. He hasn't yet given me more than I can handle."

household. Although we were a churchgoing family, looking back I realize we didn't talk much to or about God.

"My parents shocked us when they announced they were divorcing. I was twelve years old—old enough to realize it was my mother's decision. No one ever told me exactly why, just one day my dad was gone. My life changed drastically and suddenly. I didn't know anyone who had divorced parents, and since we were always taught divorce was a sin, I was ashamed—afraid someone or everyone would find out. I went as far as not inviting even my best friend to our home.

"After my father left, we saw him about once a year. My mother had a nervous breakdown shortly afterward and several unsuccessful relationships with men. I remember being afraid, often alone in the house. She would come home late at night, or sometimes not at all.

"I went on to high school, which seems like a big blur. I had three very best friends I clung to; I was too insecure to talk to boys. No one at home paid any attention to my grades or my failure notices. My mom was still living a life of partying and dating, and as a consequence, I felt unimportant and unloved. I worked to help out my mom financially since my dad wasn't paying child support (and my mom didn't have a job). Because of work, I couldn't participate in after-school activities. In many ways I was still a child; I simply felt lost. I had no idea who I was.

"Thankfully, a friend helped me apply to college. Without her I would not have gone. I went to the first college that accepted me. Those four years were tough. I drank a lot, my grades suffered, and I was promiscuous. One night I was admitted to the hospital with alcohol poisoning and my mom didn't even come visit. She laughed at the whole thing, but I never found it funny. I knew I needed help from someone, maybe even God, but prayer was the furthest thing from my mind. I never even considered communicating with God about my problems.

"Into my twenties, I focused on my career as an inner-city teacher and on my education as I earned my master's degree. But, following my mother's example, I had several unsuccessful relationships with men—one in particular lasted four years. It was a tumultuous relationship; we fought constantly and he was very critical of me. I knew we didn't share the same values, but I was determined to fix him.

"Over time, however, it was clear to me the relationship wasn't working. The years of dysfunction left me feeling unsatisfied, and I told him so over the phone while he was on a business trip. I wanted out. That night I just wept, not knowing how it had gotten to this point. I was headed in the wrong direction and didn't know how to get out. I was sad, depressed, and scared. I knelt on the floor and asked God for help. Not knowing what to say, or how to say it, I just spoke the words on my heart. 'God, I need you. I cannot do this without your help. I want to do whatever you want me to do, please help me.'

"It was immediate. After asking for God's help, I felt at peace. The grief, the pain, the fear—it honestly all melted away. I *felt* God with me. It was clear to me he was in the room and he was going to help me. I didn't know or care how; I just loved and craved the peace. I fell asleep and the next morning attended church for the first time in several years.

"As a result of my prayer time on the floor with God, I began to live differently. But I was a beginner, and I didn't realize having a relationship with God was more than just asking for help when you needed it.

"I stayed stuck spiritually in this place for many years.

"As I share with you the next chapter in my story, it may seem ironic that the catalyst for my Christian growth once again involved a man, but in retrospect, those relationships always engaged my heart. God is about the business of the heart, and so he used whatever or whoever was awakening it to speak truth to me about his love. I think those relationships and my ultimate dissatisfaction with them just mirrored my real longing, which was for greater intimacy with him. I was using men to fill a spot in my heart only God could, and I knew, deep down, they weren't enough.

"At this point I was well into my thirties, and I became engaged to a man I had dated for two years. Unfortunately, soon after the engagement, I felt unsure about marrying him. I wasn't sure if it was cold feet or legitimate doubts. I had reservations, and because I had made so many poor choices with men before, I knew I had to get this right. I didn't mention my doubts to anyone—I couldn't.

"I did not set any wedding date and friends and family started to ask questions. I told them I wasn't in a hurry, but inside I knew better. I wasn't sleeping or eating. I didn't want to make the wrong decision, and the truth was, I didn't trust myself.

"I became extremely anxious about our upcoming wedding and finally decided to turn the whole situation over to God. I began to pray—something I had stopped doing because I only thought it was for when you 'needed' God, and I hadn't needed him in a while. Every day I was begging: *God, I will do whatever you want me to do; I will marry him or end this. Show me what is your will. Please give me guidance.* I asked for some sign. Then I became angry and impatient when I couldn't see his hand, couldn't hear him.

"One night, my fiancé and I took the subway downtown for dinner. There were very few people on the train that night, but I noticed a lady sitting a few rows behind us facing ahead. She wore headphones, but I could tell she was watching us while we talked.

> "I was using men to fill a spot in my heart only God could."

"We stepped off the train and rode the escalator up to street level. This same lady was two steps ahead of us on the escalator. Suddenly she turned around and had a brief, but striking conversation with me.

"She asked if we were dating. I showed her my ring and commented that we were engaged. She looked at my fiancé and said, 'The next time I see you on this train, you will not be with her. She's going to leave you. She was talking to you and you didn't pay any attention to her. You're not giving her what she needs.'

"As she walked away, she whipped around and said, 'Who knows? Maybe this is a message from God.'

"My fiancé and I continued walking on to dinner, but I mentally stayed on the escalator. I couldn't stop thinking about the woman.

Whether or not God was speaking to me, I couldn't ignore that woman, especially when I had been begging him for a sign.

"A few days later, I called it off.

"Almost immediately sleep returned, and the anxiety vanished. I knew I had made the right decision. He answered my prayers. All of the doubts I had had were my signs, telling me something was wrong. God was speaking inside of me, and I learned a lesson from this situation that I carry with me today. Sometimes we ask for a sign in the clouds, a letter from God, and I am grateful he showed up for me so directly. I almost needed that in a season of weak faith. But most of the time in response God gives us an internal wisdom, led by the Counselor, and that counts as communication with him also. What I know for sure, what I hope for when I ask him, is that I'll get his listening ear and ready response.

"In the years since these incidents, I have developed a deeper and richer communication with God, a two-way conversation. I believe he wants to answer our pleas and prayers. I have learned that walking with God can sometimes be work. Like any relationship, it needs nurturing, and time and distraction can take its toll on our connection. Do I think he talks to me? Yes. I have experienced it and seen answered prayers. Sometimes he speaks to us through friends and family, sometimes through our priests and pastors, sometimes through strangers or music or nature, and still sometimes, it's difficult to know what he is saying at all. But I am listening and yearning to see him show up."

I finished talking to Julie and realized my world is expanding with each story. Each person opens up for me another avenue to consider as God's route of communication. It's causing me to look, listen, ask, plead, be encouraged, and ultimately to seek him in my decisions and relationships. A stranger on the subway is just the latest catalyst for me to have eyes wide open to the creator in communion with his creation.

His perspective is perfect. He can tell us from where he is sitting whether or not this person, or this job, or this move is within his will or is in our best interest. He can see the traps set for us up ahead. He can even lead us to pivot from a path thought previously right and draw us away from awaiting destruction.

How does he do that, and how can I know for sure it's him? I am hoping by straining my ear and watching for him, I will hear and see and know. To someone else it might seem like a nightmare with no meaning, or a stranger with good observational skills. But to me it feels like a beckoning finger.

13

> *In his great mercy he has given us new birth into a living hope*
> *through the resurrection of Jesus Christ from the dead, and*
> *into an inheritance that can never perish, spoil or fade.*
>
> —1 PETER 1:3, 4

I have always loved writing, and when I was working on my first manuscript, a book about our life in Mexico, I decided to do an extended fast and just finish it. During that time, I stole any moment I could to work on my laptop. Sometimes it was for as little as fifteen minutes.

One afternoon I was picking up my son Evan from soccer practice and I parked by his field. I was early and thought I could work for a few minutes. I glanced up often to see if he had noticed where I was parked, but I could tell from his searching eyes that he hadn't. Jumping out of the car, I walked briskly about twenty feet to a fence, where I shouted to get his attention. It took around four minutes before I returned to the car. When I grabbed the door handle, I gasped, then yelled out in frustration. The window was smashed and my laptop from the front seat was gone. In it (what was I thinking?) was the backup disk. The book, which I didn't have time to write in the first place, was gone.

I jumped on the roof of our Suburban, hoping to catch a glimpse of someone running away. When the locals were questioned later ("Did you see anything unusual?"), the report was filled with "The blond woman was on top of her car, standing like she was surfing...."

God's truth is found in unlikely places.

In the following months, whenever the subject of the theft came up, I would nod in agreement as people accused the enemy of stealing the book. I too would credit him with wanting to prevent the message I was writing from getting out.

What a fool.

This last year I have been studying from John's Gospel Jesus' words on the vine and the branches. How apart from him we can do nothing. How he will cut off any branch that does not bear fruit. Reading those words one hot Mexican afternoon, I felt a rush of conviction. I was writing a book full of the thoughts I had to share with others. All the wisdom and experience I had accumulated that I wanted to showcase to the world.

Vanity! No wonder that branch needed pruned.

Many months later, I checked into a hotel and picked up my new computer to begin again an outline of our story in Mexico. This time, however, it was much less about what I had to teach others and much more about what God had taught me. It was a branch that could finally now bear fruit. The joke was on the enemy—if indeed it was he who enticed someone to steal from me. At times he may look like the one with more points in his column, but he will never win. And if it seems like he is, then we need to take a step back and see/wonder/ask why the Lord decided to use him.

Crisis hits in all forms. Sometimes it's physical, sometimes it's financial, sometimes it's relational. Sometimes it feels like the whole world can see it, and other times it's very personal, with scars only we see. When everyone can see our struggle, it's easier for them to pitch in, to lower expectations of us, and to offer the benefit of the doubt. When our struggle is masked by good coping skills and high productivity, then everyone passes by, assuming the smile we plaster on our faces is sincere.

> Vanity! No wonder that branch needed pruned.

The following story offers hope that God heals all brokenness, even the kind only he can see. It also reiterates for me that everyone has a story. This story went on while many never knew it. The private wars we wage sometimes just seem easier than the cumbersome struggles everyone witnesses, but that's perception, not reality. When we walk with a crutch, people hold the door open for us. When it's just a war between our ears, or one in the space between head and heart, we aren't usually granted the space or grace to heal. Here's what happens when we are.

A BROKEN LEADER

"I didn't really want to leave. I had no idea what I would do. All I knew was something had to change; I was so stressed and so unhappy I was considering leaving the job I had loved for almost two decades. I just knew I had to get away from the unrelenting stress.

"When I approached the leadership of our organization about leaving, they told me I couldn't make this decision in the state I was in. They encouraged a sabbatical—wherever I wanted and for however long it took. I realize not everyone has this kind of authority in their vocational life. I saw it at the time as a chance to take a deep breath and would later recognize it as God's grace.

"I called some friends in San Diego who have a garage apartment. When I shared with them how much I needed to clear my head, they immediately offered me a month in the apartment, plus a car to use. Again, God was using people to pour his grace out on me.

"With the place secured, I knew I needed a plan to structure my time there, so I met with a friend, and she recommended a stack of good books and a counselor she knew in California.

"When I arrived, I quickly learned geography alone does not make you relax. I was happy to be there—could tell I needed it—but it took a full week to unwind. I thought about the past ten years and what factors had been contributing to this perfect storm.

> "With stress at work and home, I had seemingly nowhere to turn."

"Partly, my stress was a result of one of my children who had struggled with a substance addiction for four years. That is a unique kind of weight a parent carries. Only others who have walked that road understand it completely. Another piece was a different child, a really angry one, who had decided to focus his anger on me, causing us both tremendous pain. I had been feeling combative at work because I didn't always agree with the direction of our new leader. I had begun dreading the office and so had been working at home mostly. This had added to the isolation I was feeling. I started to see I had no one to talk to or laugh with, to share life with in meaningful ways.

"With stress at work and home, I had seemingly nowhere to turn.

"I was lonely.

"When you add loneliness to stress, you get a fertile ground for pain. And I was in pain. Pain I frighteningly realized I couldn't cheer myself up out of or blow off any longer. As the California days spilled into weeks, and fog began to lift from the immediate circumstances, I found out the stress was caused by far more than what I could see.

"The first book I read was *Overcoming the Dark Side of Leadership*, by Gary McIntosh and Samuel Rima. In it they talk about how every quality we have that makes us a good leader has a dark side, and if we are not aware of it and fight against it, it can destroy us. They tell stories of gifted leaders who have self-destructed because of pain or abuse in their past (Bill Clinton and Jim Bakker are among the examples). 'We are bottomless pits of need and depravity apart from Christ.' That I could understand. 'Applying the oil of grace to our lives will result in a measure of joy and freedom

OUR STORY ISN'T OVER

TTSIU is an acronym we use in our marriage, ministry, and child rearing. It stands for "time to suck it up" and came out of a particularly hot summer we had one year in Mexico. It was a non-spiritual version of "count it all loss" or "do nothing out of selfish ambition" or "do not complain, so you can shine like stars in the universe." We quote it to each other when the water bottle is warm, the bus breaks down, or the child we are holding needs a serious diaper change. It came to mind the day captured in this image, when I waited outside a less than ideal "bathroom." Sometimes life is dirty and uncomfortable. My goal these days is not fixating on my own comfort. Not squirming out of whatever is hard because I prefer easy. There are lessons and opportunities untold for me when I choose to TTSIU, there is a muscle there I want to exercise.

that will help us provide the kind of balanced leadership that will honor God, draw others to Christ and fulfill us as leaders.' This sounded good, like what I wanted, but how do you get there?

"I had one book down and a whole stack left to tackle. As I looked at the other titles, I was drawn to *How People Grow*, by Henry Cloud and John Townsend. The Lord knew this was exactly what I needed. and I spent the remainder of my time reading this one book.

"Each day I went to the beach, read my Bible and a chapter in the book, then I journaled and prayed. At the same time I saw a counselor specializing in psychodrama. As I told my story, she stopped me and commented how sad parts of my story were. The strange thing is I was sitting there telling the stories—MY stories—without emotion.

"I talked about how my dad never told me he loved me until he was eighty-five years old, lying in the hospital bed, and I said it first because I was afraid I might never see him again.

"That's sad.

"Neither of my parents hugged me when I was growing up. When I was around eight years old, I woke up crying one night because I'd had a nightmare. I called for my mom and she came in and sat on my bed and embraced me. So this is how you get hugs. After that I would pretend to have a nightmare every once in a while, just so my mom would come in and hug me.

"How sad.

"When I was twelve, my brother began acting strangely and would sometimes run away. I loved and looked up to my brother—he had taught me how to dance, how to play football and pool. He was later diagnosed with schizophrenia and sent to a state mental hospital. As usual, my parents would not talk about him and I was left in the dark. The unspoken rule in our family was 'Don't rock the boat.' There was no emotional intimacy, no honest communication, and no affection.

"Again, sad.

"Yet I was sitting there telling these stories as if they belonged to someone else. The counselor challenged me to be the little girl who never got hugged or told she was loved and to say to my parents how that felt. Wow, crazy uncomfortable. I wanted to run away, but I gave it a try. The tears flowed as I shared with my (deceased) parents how hurt and confused I was when no one held me. Then I told my brother (also deceased) how I felt when he left—how confusing and painful it was. Now there were more tears—the floodgates were open!

"I started to see how my need for control and my perfectionism, stemming from childhood pain, had brought me to the point of breaking. As a young child, I unconsciously decided that, if they were not going to love me for who I am, I would work and earn love. I became the good girl—making good grades and absolutely no trouble for anyone at all.

"The unspoken rule in our family was 'Don't rock the boat.'"

"Eventually my mental wanderings and counseling sessions hovered over my failed marriage of sixteen years, which ended when I was eight months pregnant with my third child. Even though I knew I shouldn't have gotten married when I did, I didn't know how to say so. And I had no one to talk to about it. I also believed the lie that if I didn't get married then, I would become an old maid.

"The counselor asked me to stand metaphorically at the altar and tell my husband why I couldn't marry him. Then I turned and told my parents how upset I was that they neither expressed their reservations nor provided a good example of a healthy marriage.

"So now what? I was learning a lot about myself and about God, but how would I put it all together? And how did it shape my stress level at work or with my family, and the loneliness I was experiencing? How were they related? I so wanted to be the person God originally created me to be. I wanted to experience his unconditional love and acceptance in a real, life-changing way.

"Between my reading and my counseling, my prayers and journals, I learned that I had reversed the roles as God had created them. He is the source—I depend on him (not myself). He is the creator—I am the created and cannot exist unto myself. He has control of the world. I have control of myself. He is the judge of life. I am to experience life. He designed life and its rules. I obey the rules and live the life God designed.

"*Thank you, God, for giving insight to men and women who can*

THEIR STORY ISN'T OVER

WHILE hiking in the Israeli desert with our group, Todd and I came upon a place called En Gedi—a jungle-like water oasis in the midst of a desert. En Gedi was the inspiration for Psalm 42—"As the deer pants for the water"—and Psalm 63—"Earnestly I seek you; I thirst for you, my whole being longs for you, in a dry and parched land where there is no water." We talked about how to be an En Gedi to those we love—a place where they find refreshment in an otherwise parched land. As I look at this family picture, I think the joke is really on the enemy, who tried to walk some of these girls out into the desert, and there they found En Gedi.

write about your ways and teach them in a way that makes sense.

"Every time I try to control someone or something, I play God. Every time I try to be 'perfect,' I play God. Every time I judge someone to make myself feel superior, I play God. This realization is both convicting and freeing. I started to see I had it all wrong.

"I'd always thought that if you wanted to grow spiritually, you spent more time with God, joined a Bible study, and had more quiet times. If you wanted to grow emotionally, you saw a counselor or read self-help books. But you can't separate spiritual and emotional growth; they go together. We need God and people to grow and heal.

"God continues to teach, reveal himself, convict, and most of all, love me. One day while reading verses on God's grace and love, I argued with God for over an hour: *I have no idea what unconditional love looks like. I have never experienced it from anyone—not my parents, not my husband, no one. I believe you love me unconditionally, but I don't feel it. It isn't transforming my life. I've been a Christian for thirty years. I tell people all the time about God's unconditional love and grace, but I don't really understand it.*

"Then God started speaking to me, not in an audible voice, but it was real nonetheless:

> *Didn't I prove my love for you when I sent my son, Jesus, to die on the cross for your sins? Didn't I prove my love for you when I chose you from the beginning of time and rescued you from the pit? Never forget how many prayers I have answered over the past thirty years! Your daughter is a walking miracle. She has been drug free for four years now. Look at your youngest son who is on fire for me and is growing spiritually. Look at your son who*

> Peter knew a little something about an "inheritance that can never perish, spoil or fade."

has been so hurt and angry—can you see how I am healing your relationship with him and I will continue to do so?

Look at this beautiful world I've created for you to enjoy. Look at this beach, the waves, the cliffs, the palm trees, the sand. I poured grace out on you through other people, providing places and provision for your time away. I have given you work I have gifted you to do and a heart for the lost. The people in your life may not have loved you unconditionally, but I do and I always will.

"I began praising and thanking God for his love. For the first time I could remember, I literally felt his love pour over me, and it was healing.

"Reluctantly, I watched my time away wind down, and the reality of my work life and my relationships returned. But this time when I went back, I felt more equipped to handle what came my direction. Back home I have found a group of people I can share my life with, and who ask me how I really am. It has become key to preventing a return of the private pain I had experienced earlier.

"Grace plus love plus truth in community leads to my continued healing. It works; I hear God now in ways I hadn't ever thought possible."

PETER

I have long been fascinated by Peter. So much has been written about this biblical character. He is known for his impulsive actions (water walking, ear slicing, etc.) and I know a thing or two about impulse (having tried to curb it the better part of my adult life). I have been curious lately about Peter's charisma and how both the Lord used it (Day of Pentecost) and how the enemy exploited it (his denial three times).

Peter made a disciple's career of jumping the gun and signing up for every experience. He wanted in on the healings, the feedings, the miracles. We know he was present with John when the Sadducees took Jesus in for questioning and a beating, and that he stood there within earshot of the Lord and denied he knew him.

Knowing what we do about Peter, I have tried to imagine how he handled the aftermath of his poor choice. Did he run away? seek counsel from other disciples? There are many details from those days we aren't privy to, but what I do know is ultimately the joke was on the enemy, who thought he had taken him out. After his resurrection Jesus reinstated Peter with the famous three-question exchange (John 21:15-19): "Do you love me?"

I imagine Peter's answer getting louder each time, culminating in the conviction that he does love him and will follow him, just as he asked. We know by reading more of Peter's story how critical he was in the development of the early church and those first missionary journeys. The same Lord he denied and then later died for looked at his whole life at one time and saw more than disobedience. He saw what would eventually become a defining moment in Peter's life. Peter knew a little something about an "inheritance that can never perish, spoil or fade" when he wrote his letter to the scattered believers a little later on (1 Peter 1:4).

I believe the enemy intended to take my friend out for good (if not out of her faith, then out of her vocation). He was trying to sift her, but instead she came out refined. Today she is clear-minded, surrounded by community, and at peace with her past. She enjoys a new intimacy with her Savior, and I believe she's in a long line of other Christ followers who have seen their brokenness lead to renewed strength.

I stand in that line: I have seen my doubt become resolution, my pruned branches give way for new growth, my sin lead to a greater understanding of grace, my burnout walk me into retreat (which is far more intimate than escape). The enemy sets traps for us all the time, waiting and watching for the fall. He uses our history, our present struggles, our fatigue and doubt, then adds someone else's sin and waits until we find ourselves in moments we couldn't have imagined—denying God three times or wrapped in someone else's arms or poking ourselves with a needle. And he gloats, thinking he's won.

What we can know for sure is that he couldn't be more wrong, or shortsighted.

It might seem for a moment we are lost, but like a coin that gets found and a son who comes home, we praise a God who isn't caught in the only chapter being read. He knows the ending.

Can we gain a seated-in-the-heavenlies perspective that mirrors his? Can we see missteps and/or discouragement as rocks we can stand on? Can those become not what we are embarrassed by but instead what we testify about?

14

I eagerly expect and hope that I will in no way be ashamed, but will have sufficient courage so that now as always Christ will be exalted in my body, whether by life or by death. For to me, to live is Christ and to die is gain.

—PHILIPPIANS 1:20, 21

"I don't want to be here. I don't like you. I don't like kids. I don't like heat."

A mop of blond curls sat on top of a snarling face.

I sighed and looked at him, resisting the urge to hug him.

I had heard earlier that day from his youth pastor he was sent here by his grandmother, who was worried about his grief process. He had lost his father that summer, and nothing and no one had been able to get through to him.

I wondered about the wisdom that brought him here. Would he feel trapped?

"I am sorry you feel that way." I was not sure what else to say.

His team was headed to the mountains, and so I saw him periodically throughout the day, preparing the supplies they would need for the five-day trip.

As he boarded the bus, I stopped him and told him I would be praying. It felt lame as I said it, but I wanted to say something.

"Thanks." Resigned, he offered up a half-smile.

The next five days passed in a blur, as I was busy at home. I heard the bus coming up the drive and I opened the curtains to see them pull in.

The bus blocked my view of the team descending down the stairs. I was imagining them moving slowly, tired from a long and hot drive. Instead I heard them barreling down toward the pool area and I laughed, thinking of how many miles back they must have been planning a dip in the cool water.

Ryan, one of our staff, knocked on the door and invited me to hear something special.

I followed him down to the water, where I saw everyone surrounding the sad, blond boy.

"I want to be baptized today as a symbol of my new faith," he started, looking around.

Baptized? I gasped, covered my mouth, and then smiled. Ryan whispered to me how angry the boy was when he got to the children's home. How he wasn't treating anyone very well, including the children they were there to serve. Ryan was concerned the orphans would get the wrong idea—that this boy's behavior reflected them—so he told them a bit about this boy's traumatic summer.

"This isn't a testimony of how God made all things right in the end—it's more a story of immeasurable grace."

As children who have lived for a lifetime with loss and without one or more parents, they were moved with compassion and determined among themselves to be agents of God's love to him. They purposed together to reverse the mission trip and serve this boy, praying for and reaching out to him. They sang near him, laid hands on him, and worked alongside him. In the end, it was their testimony that led to his own.

"Thank you for bearing with me and seeing me to this," he

finished, and his voice caught. His pastor spared him more words and placed a hand on his back and one over his chest. Together they bent down, breaking the surface of the water and identifying with the death and then resurrection of Jesus Christ.

Applause broke out around the pool.

Extracting preciousness from worthlessness is never more difficult than when it involves children. There is something innate in us that wants to protect them; and the smaller the child, the fiercer that instinct. We get that from Jesus, who threatens those who come against children with millstones around their necks. We read that he welcomed them onto his lap and healed them on many occasions. It's why we can go to him when there's trouble with our own children, knowing our prayers will move his hand. I can only imagine how strong the presence of Christ himself was in the room during the following events.

NICK

"Most people bring their children into the world with few problems, but for others the journey opens up an array of emotions and anguish that they would have never imagined. Our journey with Nicholas was a long walk, and at times we stumbled and fell, but this isn't a testimony of how God made all things right in the end—it's more a story of immeasurable grace.

"My wife, Jenny, and I always dreamed of a large family. I wanted twelve kids, and she agreed so long as I had six and she had six. When our son, Alex, was sixteen, and our daughters Allison and Leah were five and one-and-a-half, we were thrilled to learn we were expecting again. Since all of the previous pregnancies had been relatively normal, we didn't foresee any trouble with this pregnancy either. Things were going well and at twenty weeks, Jenny went for an ultrasound to find out the sex of the baby.

"'It's a boy!' We were elated.

"Then the technician remarked, 'Wait here, something doesn't look right.' And we don't remember breathing until the doctor came in and spoke, with a perplexed look on her face, 'It appears your son has a diaphragmatic hernia.'

"Jenny and I looked at each other with fear. I didn't know what that was, but it didn't sound good. The doctor took a moment to explain that our baby's diaphragm did not close completely, but should be able to be fixed. Her words made it sound like everything was going to be OK. We listened to her numbly and kept it together in the office, but as soon as we left, we started to pray. *God, you've got this—right?*

"The next week we went to see the specialist and were not at all prepared for (who is?) 'Your son has about a 50/50 chance of survival.' After explaining the experimental procedures being done to fix the defect and the success rates involved, the doctor looked at us both and asked sincerely, 'Are you considering terminating the pregnancy?'

Jenny and I with tears in our eyes looked first at each other. Gathering conviction, I said to him, 'No, abortion is not an option. We do not believe in abortion.'

"It felt good to say it so forcibly. Abortion had gone from being a policy or a position to hold to a viable way out of this situation. But we both knew in our hearts we could not turn our backs on God or his ways. He would bring us through this, somehow.

"The specialist gave us some very vague information about our son's (we named him Nick) condition, and said he would see us in a couple of months. In the meantime, they would get an MRI, and we would tour the neonatal intensive care unit at Children's Hospital. We mumbled our thanks, paid at the door, and stumbled our way to the car. I wish I could say in this moment, I was a strong Christian man. That my faith held up like a rock, and everyone in my family clung to it. But instead, the truth is, a thousand lies, a thousand negative thoughts all began assaulting my mind.

"On the ride home, Jenny and I cried, but did not say much.

"I was angry, particularly at God. How could he let this happen? I had turned my life back over to him and was being faithful. How could he be doing this to Jenny and me? We loved him so much. I thought maybe this was a punishment for turning away from him earlier and not being faithful to the call he had placed on my life. All I could think at this point, over and over and over and over again was why? *Why, Lord?*

> "Your son has about a 50/50 chance of survival."

"When we got home, Jenny and I were more ready to talk, and we tried to encourage one another by praying and reading Scripture aloud. We didn't know (and still don't) why this was happening, but we knew God would be faithful and bring us through it. Months followed, filled with testing and appointments, and while we both prayed for the best, we prepared for the worst. During this season, we educated ourselves on Nick's condition and grimly made funeral arrangements. His birth, which meant the culmination of all our hopes and plans, was scheduled for November 4, 2004.

"'It's a boy!' Those words reminded me of the first time I heard them at the ultrasound. For a few moments, time was suspended, and everything floated in the room. Nicholas was born, and to my eyes, the lay eyes of his father, all seemed fine.

HIS STORY ISN'T OVER

This is a picture of my friend, Brian, who visits here frequently in Monterrey. The children, hungry for male attention, respond to even the smallest gesture of affection. The role of fathers is critical in a child's life, yet somehow when we ask more of men, we give them less credit for their efforts. I want to celebrate what men offer to this movement. Their energy, protection, and care cover many orphans around the world. I am thankful Brian stopped his work project on this day to swing this child around. I am thankful he is using his strength for this God-ordained adventure.

"But the dream stopped abruptly, as they whisked him away, nurses and doctors and monitors and noises in his wake. Looking back, I do thank God for the miracle of modern medicine. Without it, that would have been my only encounter with our son.

"I glanced down at Jenny, and she knew as I prepared to leave and follow Nick to Children's Hospital, that I was going for both of us. We had prepared for this, talked about this. God's grace was beginning to cover the words and emotions I couldn't even name.

"I saw Nick again in an isolation room, and he was hooked up to all kinds of machines. I couldn't help it, it seemed, the anger at God welled up again strong in my flesh. It felt at once odd, because I remembered we had made peace with him and this situation. But apparently not. I don't think I was fully prepared for what was happening.

"My faith, all that it amounted to, was shaking at its core. What did I believe about life? death? his promises? his provision? What was his responsibility to me? to Nick? What role did I play in that? did my faith play? Could I change the situation? Could I pray more? believe more? ask more? I can't imagine so; I had been doing that now for months.

"I stood in that hospital room with God, my son, and a bunch of strangers. Even though I knew God was with me, I have never felt more alone.

"I watched them manipulate the machines, doctors speaking to me words about stabilization and 24-48 hours. Then it hit me. They were trying to keep Nick alive long enough so that my wife could make it to the hospital and say good-bye. Another wave of grief came over me. How many of these could I stand up under? I just stood there, tears streaming down my face, as the doctor tried his best to explain the situation.

"I left the hospital that night, feeling hurt, brokenhearted, and neglected. I know it's not true, but it felt as though God did not care about me or my family or what we were going through. *What do I pray, Lord, when I don't even know if you care?*

> "Even though I knew God was with me, I have never felt more alone."

"Nick surprised us all, and beating the odds, surpassed his expiration date (given to us by the doctors). The next few days and weeks were a roller coaster of emotions. My faith buoyed as the situation was moving in our favor. It motivated us and those surrounding us to be in continuous prayer, and that held our family together.

"For me, prayer kept me from believing that we would lose Nick. He would be doing well one day and then not so well the next. His condition would go from bad, to really bad, to not as bad.

"Once Nick was stabilized, they decided that it would be best to put him on a heart-lung bypass machine. This machine would act as his heart and lungs, giving his body some much needed rest. The only downside was that a person could be on it no longer than fourteen days. I called the prayer chain and had people praying, just as before. This is how I knew that my faith was still working, because in spite of what I was feeling, I kept on praying and asking God for his help. I knew the situation and this boy were in hands bigger than mine. Nick was on the machine for thirteen days.

"The next step was surgery to repair Nick's diaphragm. His stomach, both intestines, his liver, and his spleen were all in his chest cavity. Since all organs were in his chest, this did not allow for his lungs to develop, as seen by the fetal MRI. All X-rays indicated that Nick did not have much of either lung. The left was almost nonexistent, and the right could not be seen at all. How could he live without lungs?

"God! What are you up to?"

"After the surgery, the doctor said Nick had almost a full right lung, and a quarter of his left. The doctor said the X-rays probably just couldn't detect them because of the organs in the way. I didn't buy that for a minute, but when you don't believe in God, you have to have some kind of explanation. There was never a doubt to those who believed; we were witnessing a miracle of God unfold before our eyes. God was moving in this body, making a way where there wasn't one!

"We were still far from being out of the woods, but I started at this point to entertain thoughts of being able to take Nick home. We had been at Children's Hospital NICU for almost two and a half months.

"Nick did not have room in his abdomen for all of his organs, so for several weeks part of his intestines were in a plastic silo on top of his abdomen, until his abdomen grew and the intestines fell into place. A skin graft was done to close his abdomen. Then something remarkable was discovered that could not be explained medically—his left lung began to grow. The chief of the NICU, whose specialty was diaphragmatic hernias, told us point-blank this does not happen, and there was no known medical explanation for it.

"*God! What are you up to?*

"My wife and I remained faithful in prayer. We were with our son every moment we could be. We were usually the first parents there and the last to leave at night. We took turns staying in the Ronald McDonald House, in this city not our own. Jenny would stay a few nights, and then I would stay a few nights, allowing our children to live a somewhat normal life at home. Jenny and I would spend most of our time praying, singing praises, and reading Scripture to our son. The nurses would spend lots of time in our room. The chaplain would come by often; he spent so much time with us that our next son, Cooper, was named after him.

"There was one doctor in particular that would spend a lot of time in Nick's room. I would often catch the doctor doing his work in Nick's room, and he would apologize sheepishly. I understood completely. There was something about Nick, about the presence felt in his room. You couldn't explain it, but people just wanted to be with him.

"Once he was taken off the respirator, he began to smile. There were many times a small crowd would be in his room, and he would just look at everyone and smile, like he didn't have a care in the world. Things at this point were starting to look good.

"The doctors set milestones for Nick to reach in order to come home. I returned home from my days that week with him with sincere hope in my heart, and it felt so good. I thought my faith was paying off, and God was truly working a miracle.

"'Nick is not himself.' Jenny's call interrupted my thoughts. I could hear her concern. I didn't think that much of it—I had just been there, things were looking up. I refused to doubt.

"'Something is wrong, Brian. They're putting his chest tubes back in; he is draining fluid from his lungs. Pray!' I felt threatened, my swelling faith felt threatened, my son felt threatened.

"A temporary life spent on earth does not thwart God's overall plan."

"*God! Keep my head above this water!*

"I hesitated at 11:00 PM to make our good-night call. What would she say? When she answered, my heart sank. 'Something is very wrong. Come to Columbus now.'

"I barely remember that call, or taking the kids to my in-laws, or the frantic drive from our home, over an hour away. I tried to call Jenny numerous times on my way up. The staff at the hospital would not let me talk to her. Each time I tried to call, I would turn off the radio so that I could hear. The last time I called, the nurse told me to get there as quickly as possible. It was after midnight. I knew that something was terribly wrong. I turned on the radio and heard the song "Dancing with Angels." My heart broke, and I knew my son had passed away.

"There was no preparation for the reality I would find at the hospital. The news ripped through me like a bullet. My son, who had come so far, was gone. I so desperately wanted him to be healed, but God had other plans. I waited, anticipating the anger I hated, but that had reared itself at less painful moments than this.

But instead in its place, I felt a peace. It was a peace that I did not understand. I so wanted to be angry with God again, but I couldn't. I wanted to blame him for all of this, but couldn't. God was there holding me up. I could feel him.

HIS STORY ISN'T OVER

I was standing in this area of Mexico one morning, looking around at the tremendous need and thinking through one of my favorite verses, Psalm 91:1: "Whoever dwells in the shelter of the Most High will rest in the shadow of the Almighty." I am working towards a purer theology, one that allows the *shelter* definition to be as true for this man in the picture as it is for me. Do I expect God to shelter me with a nice roof over my head or great relationships around me? Or could I learn to desire the shadow lands (where he offers rest) as much as I want the land of plenty?

"The next couple of days were a whirlwind until Nick's funeral. People who never even met Nick were there. My friends, coworkers, and members of our church were all there. I was shocked to see the church doors open and in walk more than twenty staff from the hospital, including one doctor and his wife, all who had made the hour-long trip to say good-bye to Nick. My chaplain friend, Gary Cooper, pulled me aside and said he had never seen so many staff at a funeral. Nick, even though he had never said a word, had touched so many lives.

"God used Nick to draw people to him, and today, for me, that is OK. I know God has a plan for Nick's life. A plan that spans from the beginning of time throughout all eternity. A temporary life spent on earth does not thwart God's overall plan for Nick. He was still created for his glory. My faith has been tested; it went through the fire, and the parts that were not of him were burned off, painfully so. I wrestled with him, and argued and questioned, but never gave up, never turned my back on him. And as a result, Nick and I have a testimony to share. A story of how God used a baby to touch a community, draw together a family, and refine the faith of his father."

For me, extracting precious from the worthless never seems as sharply defined as it does when we talk about death. I first heard the verse used in this context during a funeral for a dear family friend who took his own life. It was all so senseless and confusing, and the family was huddled together in the front row with their lifetime of memories and hope deferred. There stood a pastor in front of them, with the great responsibility of speaking words of comfort and wisdom:

> *Why has my pain been perpetual*
> *And my wound incurable, refusing to be healed?*
> *. . .*
> *Therefore, thus says the LORD,*
> *"If you return, then I will restore you—*
> *Before Me you will stand;*
> *And if you extract the precious from the worthless,*
> *You will become My spokesman.*
> *. . .*
> *Then I will make you to this people*
> *A fortified wall of bronze;*
> *And though they fight against you,*

They will not prevail over you;
For I am with you to save you
And deliver you," declares the LORD.
(Jeremiah 15:18-20, *NASB*)

It was the most sincere exchange I had ever witnessed between the hurting and a comforter. It did not smack of spiritual platitudes. He did not try to make them feel or sense or accept that this was for anyone's good. These words expressed what we were all thinking: *This is worthless! A life lost is tragic!* Then they went on to reassure us—pain will not prevail, delivery is imminent, and something precious would and could be born out of this current pain. It's a storyline only Heaven can read.

For the blond-haired boy who lost his father, his dad's death will never be separated from his own rebirth. For Brian and Jenny, Nick's life solidified their faith, enriched their lives, and drew others into their family and faith community. Who but God can make something sweet linger after the sting of death?

15

*Do not despise these small beginnings, for the
LORD rejoices to see the work begin.*

—ZECHARIAH 4:10

As a little girl (and as a big one) I had some big ideas.
Big, ridiculous, unrealistic, expensive ideas. As a child, I would wait
for my dad to come home, some-
times meeting him in the garage,
and without a greeting I would
launch into my pitch. The "sale"
would start with a passionate argument on how this idea would
make things better for all of us or at least someone. He would listen, ask clarifying questions, and then finish almost always with the
same phrase: "Scope and timing, Beth." It wasn't that the idea du
jour was bad, but he started trying to teach me from a young age
that success depends on scaling the idea to my current reality.

> "Scope and timing,
> Beth."

I think that's why I love this verse so deeply: "Do not despise
these small beginnings, for the LORD rejoices to see the work begin" (Zechariah 4:10). It speaks to the process and not just the
result. It announces how much God values the next step as much
as the final one.

All the people I interviewed, at some point, hit a moment when
they felt the water come over their heads and the threat of their
circumstances drowning them. It was in that moment—when they

heard, "Kick! Swim! Move! You are still here!"—that they took their first small steps. Their stories didn't turn around immediately (and some still haven't.) But they are moving, walking, growing. They are believing, hoping, trusting. Success is measured with intuition, understanding scope and timing.

———

When Todd and I arrived in Mexico in 1997, we didn't know anything, didn't have any big plan, didn't speak Spanish—we were just moving in the direction of what felt like a big call. By the end of the first week we had run out of cash. We had brought the rest of our money over the border, enough for what we hoped was one year, in traveler's checks.

"Do not despise these small beginnings."

We found a bank on that day and waited patiently in line until it was our turn in front of the thick glass window. I slid some checks under the glass and smiled.

Surely she understands without my talking that I want the equivalent in pesos, right?

The lady slid them back to me and said loudly, "*Tienesquefirmartunombreaqui. . . .*" I had no idea what she'd said, let alone meant. I smiled and pushed them back to her, rubbing my thumb and fingers together—the universal sign for money, right?

She looked annoyed (no language required there) and slid them back to me, this time speaking loudly into her microphone, "*Firmetunombre!*"

I shrugged, looking sheepish. *I got nothing.*

"TU. NOMBRE. FIRME. TU. NOMBRE."

This time, with the emphatic pauses, I could tell it was several words strung together, and I excitedly said to Todd, "I heard *nombre*. I know that word!" I proceeded to take out a piece of paper and, to confirm I had heard correctly, I printed out the word *NOMBRE*. Then looking at her questioningly, I showed her my paper through the glass.

Rolling her eyes and motioning to the long line forming behind me, she nodded, "Si, *nombre*." And she pointed to a line at the bottom of the check, pushing them back to me.

I eagerly and neatly printed out "N-O-M-B-R-E" on the line (signing the word name on the signature line, instead of actually signing my name).

She finally laughed at my blunder, called over the bilingual manager, and we straightened it all out. I am sure they still laugh about me to this day.

"Do not despise these small beginnings."

Today, our organization has an operational budget in the millions of dollars and stewards rupees, pesos, dollars, and naira. God saw all of that yet to come when he watched me botch that first bank transaction.

He sees our whole lives at one time. He sees how the first step toward forgiveness will lead to a freedom we can't imagine yet in our future. He sees how a flicker of hope will become a blaze of confidence later. He sees how a deep breath today is a small step toward survival tomorrow.

We have so many choices on this journey. We have choices to give up (on ourselves or others) or to keep going. To bring more pain to exposed wounds or to be the one who doesn't kick someone who's already down. To be vulnerable and create connection in our relationships or to maintain an artificial façade and keep a distance.

Wherever we are on our faith journey, God knows and sees it all. He sees the chapters already experienced and the chapters yet to come. He has great expectations for us and yet infinite grace. He sets the bar impossibly high and then carries us there in his arms.

> There are people all over this globe who are waking up today and choosing relentless hope.

I am covenanting with Christ to see more than what is on the surface. I am a woman determined to risk my reputation if God asks me to walk in a direction others don't understand (or agree with).

I will set my eyes on the things above.

I will be seated in the heavenlies, even if I have to climb up there anew every day because I wake up forgetting how good it feels.

I am leaning in (like a girl on tiptoes), believing the rejoicing for life I feel inside has a source bigger than me.

There are people all over this globe who are waking up today and choosing relentless hope. They are facing natural disasters and personal ones. They are in debt or unemployed or enslaved. They are hungry or in pain or just plain tired.

And they are looking up instead of out.

They are exercising a relentless kind of hope. Since I have started looking, I have found countless examples, only a fraction of which I have shared in this book. It's a mark of the believer—not that we won't have troubles, but that whatever they may be, they won't overcome us.

In Exodus, after the plagues had devastated the land, and after the Red Sea had closed in on the chasing Egyptians, and after the Israelites had finally been freed from Pharaoh's hand, Moses and his people gathered around in worship on the dry side of freedom. In 15:20, 21 (*NLT*), we read: "Then Miriam the prophet, Aaron's sister, took a tambourine and led all the women as they played their tambourines and danced. And Miriam sang this song: 'Sing to the LORD, for he has triumphed gloriously; he has hurled both horse and rider into the sea.'"

Don't you find it curious that as these women were fleeing their houses with nothing more than what they could carry, and as they were passing through the parted waters—walking with their babies, the sick, the elderly, some food, a family heirloom or two—that they didn't drop the nonessential *tambourines*? What made them grab them as they were racing out the door, anyway?

They had faith. An expectation that a worship service was imminent. *We might need our tambourines.*

I am wondering how often I drop my tambourine (in the hustle

THEIR STORY ISN'T OVER

IN the end, we are all the same. A mess. A big, beautiful, ridiculous mess. Some of our messes leave outwardly visible signs, and some no one ever sees. I am working on hugging the people who cross my path. Hugging and loving more, and judging less. I am trying to see adults as just children with more days under their belts and fancier clothes, because children can be less intimidating to reach out to, and easier to be less critical of. There's a reason God sums up the whole law with words on love . . . it really does cover a multitude of sins.

and bustle of leaving the house in a hurry and running through the parted waters), forgetting, or worse yet, doubting that there will be something ahead to celebrate. I want to live more often like Miriam and her Jewish sisterhood, poised and ready for the moment when it is time to break out in song.

This is where we started this conversation, with a core belief that there are tambourine-waving moments to be captured along the way in everyone's story. A conviction that we shouldn't wait until the end, holding our breath, wondering if we will have something to praise God for. I have a feeling those women grabbed their tambourines because they had them within arm's reach. They must have been celebrating with each plague—God's provision, their spared sons, their sense of community, their impending freedom, and the many moments in the journey when they had already felt God's presence.

> "God used an unplanned pregnancy to jolt me back to truth."

DADDY'S GIRL

As I have shared the content of this book with others, I have been amazed at the stories I continually hear. Stories that were meant to take us out, but instead strengthened us. One final example comes from a Facebook friend, who willingly offered up her "testimony of the process" in a recent message to me.

"I grew up a pastor's only daughter in the Bible belt, a real daddy's girl. The summer before my senior year in high school, I traveled with my youth group on my first mission trip. In love with the Lord, I was eager to get into a Christian college and go about doing the

Lord's work. On returning from my trip, I was met by my heart-broken mother, who shared the hard truth that my father had been unfaithful for the last year. She had suffered silently, not wanting to take away from the blur of college tours and the mission trip I had been looking forward to.

"Stunned, my initial response was to pray.

"As the shock wore off, the enemy took hold of what my dad had done and used it to shatter my heart and my perception of men, and then distort my connection to my Father in Heaven.

"So with that confusion, I went off to a Christian college and my life was a fake, angry, trashy mess. I immersed myself in sin—smoking, getting high or drunk, staying out all night at clubs and sleeping through classes. I was rebelling with abandon while working as a youth ministry intern at a local church. I was the worst kind of person, because I was proclaiming Christ and living a lie.

"I was so deceived by Satan's lies, I didn't even realize how fake I was.

"God used an unplanned pregnancy to jolt me back to truth. It was more than a decade ago now, but I can still see how in God's merciful, tender, gracious way, he used a beautiful baby girl and the love I immediately had for her to remind me that I too am his child, and I am loved by him.

"What my own life wasn't worth to me in terms of protecting, hers was. Through that experience and the unbelievable support my mother gave us, God brought me back to a place where my heart was eager to be healed. Eventually, I was able to forgive my father (and see his life and ministry restored, by God's grace) and be a daddy's girl again.

"Today, God has blessed me with a wonderful husband, who is honorable and strong and trustworthy, and we are blending our families and grateful for the children we have together.

"I tried to walk away, and God let me go a certain distance. But prayers and history and faith and grace walked me back to the cross and into fellowship with him.

"Of all the consequences my lifestyle should have brought with it, in God's mercy, he blessed me with my daughter as an avenue of heart change. She is strong and resilient, a beautiful young lady who understands the Lord's work in her life. I can't wait to keep watching his story for her life unfold!"

I am waking up more days (my better ones) asking God for a story.

I had so many questions for her. "When did your mom become supportive?" "How/when did your father repent?" "How did the church come around you or reject you during your pregnancy?" "How much does your daughter know?"

I am curious about the story, because this process has changed me to become story-oriented. I want to hear about the moments in the middle, the little ways she began to see God as he intercepted her path. He doesn't stop showing up, we just stop looking. So when did she notice him again? What did/does he whisper to her, over her? What small steps did she begin to take toward turning her attitude and life around? When did she realize he was rejoicing "to see the work begin"?

I am waking up more days (my better ones) asking God for a story.

That is meaning more spontaneity in my day, more I-don't-know-where-this-is-leading-but-what-does-it-hurt-to-find-out?

I had a meeting yesterday with our local children's services about a program they are starting for pregnant teens. It turned out the meeting went a different direction, and we ended up talking about a specific child of an orphan. An orphan of an orphan (of most likely, an orphan). Chould I be frustrated? Should I say no because I felt tricked/confused and it's just easier to "set boundaries"? Or instead can I say, "Lord, what are you up to? I am all in. Can't wait to read the next chapter."

As a result of that attitude shift, I am going to possibly play a part in a little five-month-old boy and his future. Now that's a much more interesting story than the one I went there chasing.

When a plan is disrupted, or a plane missed, I am asking more and more, "What story is waiting for me?" Seeing my days like pages to be turned, and my seasons like chapters, makes me OK with the plot twists or character development. Those are the best stories, the ones where we wait and watch for what's going to happen next, that leave us in suspense, or have a host of "bad guys." The movies we cry in, because the emotion runs deep. The protagonists we cheer for, because they overcome.

This book is full of characters I can cheer for. I want to tell their stories because they inspire me to live my life more intentionally.

They inspire me to engage.

I wonder about the "great cloud of witnesses" talked about in Hebrews 11. I think because I know a few people up there in that cloud, I wonder who and what they cheer us on towards. They all had such great stories, you can read in this chapter about familiar names and characters, and I'm guessing you know a few not record-ed in the Scriptures. But my favorite part of that chapter is the end, where it says (vv. 32-40):

And what more shall I say? I do not have time to tell about Gideon, Barak, Samson and Jephthah, about David and Samuel and the prophets, who through faith conquered kingdoms, administered justice, and gained what was promised; who shut the mouths of lions, quenched the fury of the flames, and escaped the edge of the sword; whose weakness was turned to strength; and who became powerful in battle and routed foreign armies. Women received back their dead, raised to life again. There were others who were tortured, refusing to be released so that they might gain an even better resurrection. Some faced jeers and flogging, and even chains and imprisonment. They were put to death by stoning; they were sawed in two; they were killed by the sword. They went about in sheepskins and goatskins, destitute, persecuted and mistreated—the world was not worthy of them. They wandered in deserts and mountains, living in caves and in holes in the ground.

These were all commended for their faith, yet none of them received what had been promised, since God had planned something better for us so that only together with us would they be made perfect.

I think the ultimate extraction of precious from worthless happens on the other side of eternity, when it will all make sense—the good, the hard, it will make perfect sense. We will finally have the perspective we can only dabble in here. I can't wait to ask them about their stories, and I can't wait to share mine. I want to hear for an eternity about how one person's story inspired another's. It's going to be amazing to hear the stories spoken from the mouth of the Storyweaver and see how one plot bled into another.

I can't wait.

The stories in this book are just more examples. Today in your church body, perhaps in your family or among your friends, someone has been knocked out and is down for the count. Today I have a friend in the hospital with a chronically ill child, another friend whose daughter isn't valuing her own life. Today I have a friend unhappy in a marriage and another undergoing cancer surgery this week. I have a teenager with an attitude and another friend in debt. I, myself, have had disappointments, conflicts, irritations, and just plain sin rampant in my week. I cannot be alone. I don't have exceptionally dysfunctional friends, I just live in a world hell-bent on destruction.

> *Do not call to mind the former things,*
> *Or ponder things of the past.*
> *Behold, I will do something new,*
> *Now it will spring forth;*
> *Will you not be aware of it?*
> *I will even make a roadway in the wilderness,*
> *Rivers in the desert. . . .*
> *I have given waters in the wilderness*
> *And rivers in the desert,*
> *To give drink to My chosen people.*
> *The people whom I formed for Myself*
> *Will declare My praise.*
> *(Isaiah 43:18-21, NASB)*

No matter the desert, no matter the wilderness, there is nowhere we can wander off to, no land where the heat is too strong, nowhere God can't make a roadway or a river of living water to refresh us.

God is doing something new. The story may look grim, but he's turning the page. What are my choices?

Despair. Discouragement. Anger.

Self-pity. Self-righteousness. Self-destruction.

Or.

Faith. Grace. Joy.

In others, with others, in and with myself, in God.

Hope.

For a lifeline, for a bigger picture, for a heavenly purpose, for what we need exactly on time.

I will lean in. I will stand up. I will reach out. I will hope.

Relentlessly.

ABOUT THE AUTHOR

BETH GUCKENBERGER

After graduating from Indiana University in 1994, Beth returned for a short stint to her hometown of Cincinnati, Ohio, where she was a public school teacher. In 1997, she and her husband, Todd, began working with Back2Back Ministries, a leader in the field of orphan care and child development. Since then, Beth has traveled to speak to many churches, schools, and universities about the church's role in the orphan crisis and about the stories of redemption, unconditional love, and hope she and others have experienced through their encounters with the ministry. In 2008, Beth's first book, *Reckless Faith*, was published. *New York Times* bestselling author Karen Kingsbury said, "For those among us who feel led to care for orphans . . . *Reckless Faith* offers priceless insight."

Beth and Todd serve as executive directors of Back2Back Ministries, which is still headquartered in Cincinnati, Ohio. Currently, their ministry has operations in three different countries (Mexico, India, and Nigeria). They moved to Monterrey, Mexico, in 1997 and since that time have hosted thousands of guests on their ministry campus. They are also parents to nine children (three biological, three through adoption, and three through long-term foster care).

Besides speaking at church services, conferences, and retreats, Beth is a guest speaker for NASCAR, has participated on KLOVE cruises, and is the keynote speaker for the women's conference at the 2011 North American Christian Convention. Beth also contributes regularly to a blog for her ministry at back2backministries.wordpress.com. In every forum, Beth's passion is communicating how God is writing the story of her life, and how he is still working in the lives of many whose testimonies "don't have a bow on them."

Learn more about *Relentless Hope* at
www.standardpub.com/relentlesshope

Do you share a passion for the orphan child?

Beth and Todd Guckenberger are co-leaders for Back2Back Ministries, an international Christian non-profit organization that is dedicated to being a voice for orphans. Back2Back exists to love and care for orphans and impoverished children, by meeting their physical, spiritual, educational, social and emotional needs. Our desire is to share with them a God who has loved and planned for them since before they were born.

We Invite You to Join Us...

- Go on a mission trip
- Sponsor a child
- Invite Beth to speak at an event

For More Information...

- Check out our blog at www.back2backministries. wordpress.com
- Find us on Facebook
- Email us at relentlesshope@ back2backministries.org

BACK 2 BACK
M I N I S T R I E S

www.back2back.org
P.O. Box 70, Mason, OH 45040
513.754.0300